职通中文
Access to Vocational Chinese

畜禽生产技术

Livestock and Poultry Production Technology

郁云峰 总主编
于天琪 谭方正 龙杰 副总主编
山东畜牧兽医职业学院 编

初级篇
Elementary

中国教育出版传媒集团
高等教育出版社·北京

图书在版编目（C I P）数据

职通中文．畜禽生产技术．初级篇 / 郁云峰总主编 ；于天琪，谭方正，龙杰副总主编 ；山东畜牧兽医职业学院编．-- 北京 ：高等教育出版社，2025．3．-- ISBN 978-7-04-063543-0

Ⅰ．H195．4

中国国家版本馆 CIP 数据核字第 2024F8Y639 号

ZHITONG ZHONGWEN CHUQIN SHENGCHAN JISHU CHUJIPIAN

策划编辑 李 玮　　责任编辑 蔡 丹　　封面设计 张 楠　　版式设计 张丽南

责任校对 熊世钰　　责任印制 高 峰

出版发行 高等教育出版社

社　　址 北京市西城区德外大街 4 号

邮政编码 100120

印　　刷 固安县铭成印刷有限公司

开　　本 787mm×1092mm　1/16

印　　张 19

字　　数 298 千字

购书热线 010-58581118

咨询电话 400-810-0598

网　　址 http://www.hep.edu.cn

http://www.hep.com.cn

网上订购 http://www.hepmall.com.cn

http://www.hepmall.com

http://www.hepmall.cn

版　　次 2025 年 3 月第 1 版

印　　次 2025 年 3 月第 1 次印刷

定　　价 108.00 元

物 料 号　63543-00

编写委员会

总 主 编：郁云峰

副总主编：于天琪　谭方正　龙　杰

主　　编：杜文萍　张广斌

副 主 编：李晓翠　吴欣玉

编　　者：宋新宇　王柯萌　郑宏宇　郭志有　刘　青　李朝云

编辑委员会

主　　　任：肖　琼　孙云鹏

项目负责人：李　玮　盛梦晗

项 目 编 辑：李欣欣　杨　漾　陆姗娜　蔡　丹　熊世钰

专家委员会（按音序排列）

陈曼倩　哈尔滨职业技术大学

梁赤民　中国-赞比亚职业技术学院

刘建国　哈尔滨职业技术大学

宋　凯　有色金属工业人才中心

赵丽霞　有色金属工业人才中心

崔永华　北京语言大学

梁　宇　北京语言大学

宋继华　北京师范大学

苏英霞　北京语言大学

前 言

为进一步推动各国学习者中文语言能力和专业技能深度融合，提升学习者围绕特定行业场景、典型工作任务使用中文进行沟通和交流的能力，持续满足中文学习者的职业规划和个人发展需求，实现优质教育资源共享，促进多彩文明交流互鉴，教育部中外语言交流合作中心联合有色金属工业人才中心，根据各国“中文＋职业技能”教学发展实际需求，以中国职业院校为依托，组织职业教育、国际中文教育、出版和相关企业等领域的专家，共同研发了“职通中文”系列教材及其配套教学资源。

“职通中文”系列教材参照《国际中文教育中文水平等级标准》和《职业中文能力等级标准》，分为初、中、高三个等级。各等级均遵循“语言和技能相融合”“好学、好教、好用”的编写理念，依据相关职业的典型工作场景、工作任务和高频用语，设计课文、会话、语言点和练习等板块，不断提升学习者在职业技术领域的中文应用水平和关键技术能力，为学习者尽快熟悉和适应工作环境提供帮助。本系列教材适用于在中资企业从事相关职业的各国员工，同样适用于在华留学生或长短期培训人员，也适用于有意向了解中国语言文化和职业技能的学习者。

《职通中文 畜禽生产技术 初级篇》是“职通中文”系列教材之一，适用于在海外中资企业从事畜禽生产相关岗位的本土员工。通过本教材，学习者能够用中文进行简单的工作交流，掌握从新员工进出养殖场安全规定到圈舍的清理、消毒，再到管理畜禽的基本操作。

本教材在编写过程中，参照《畜牧兽医专业教学标准》，聘请畜牧行业专家把关，调研驻外中资企业，了解企业对从业人员的语言、技能及总体素质要求，将实际工作场景和典型工作任务中的真实语料，编写成符合“零基础”学习者水平的课文和对话。全书共30课，每课包括复习、热身、生词、课文、语法、汉字、拓展和小结等八个部分，同时配有图片，力求以图文并茂的形式呈现真实的职业场景。此外还配套开发了音频、视频等资源，帮助学习者掌握在职业场景中用中文进行基本交际的能力。

学习者学习本教材后应当可以：

1. 具备基本的中文理解和运用能力，为职场应用和中文进阶学习打下基础；
2. 掌握畜禽生产工作中常用的基本词汇、专业术语及常用表达，并应用到日常交际及工作岗位中；
3. 对中国文化具有基本的理解和认识，能够注意到与中国客户沟通交流时的文化差异，提升职业竞争力。

本书得到了教育部中外语言交流合作中心、有色金属工业人才中心和专家组的支持，我们在此表示衷心感谢。本书还得益于高等教育出版社的鼎力支持和精心指导，在此一并致谢。

“职通中文”系列教材的出版和应用旨在促进各国“中文＋职业技能”人才的培养，助力当地经济发展，从而为构建人类命运共同体做出积极贡献。由于项目团队学识和相关经验有限，加之时间紧迫，本书肯定有许多疏漏、不足有待完善。恳请本书的使用者将发现的问题反馈给我们，以便再版和编写相关教材时改进。

本书编写组

2024年10月

Preface

In order to further promote the deep integration of Chinese language proficiency and professional skills among learners from various countries and enhance their ability to communicate and interact in Chinese in specific industry scenarios and typical work tasks, the Center for Language Education and Cooperation under the Ministry of Education, in collaboration with China Nonferrous Metal Industry Talent Center, has organized experts from vocational education, international Chinese education, publishing, and related enterprises to jointly develop the "Access to Vocational Chinese" series of textbooks and supporting teaching resources. Based on the actual needs of "Chinese + Vocational Skills" teaching development in various countries and relying on Chinese vocational colleges, the series aims to continuously meet the career planning and personal development needs of Chinese learners, realize the sharing of high-quality educational resources, and promote exchanges and mutual learning among diverse civilizations.

In reference to the *Chinese Proficiency Grading Standards for International Chinese Language Education* and the *Chinese Proficiency Standards for Vocational Education*, the "Access to Vocational Chinese" series of textbooks is divided into three levels: elementary, intermediate, and advanced. All levels follow the writing philosophy of "integrating language and skills" and "being easy to learn, teach, and use." The textbooks are designed around typical work scenarios, work tasks, and high-frequency terms of relevant professions, with sections on texts, conversations, language points, and exercises, continuously improving learners' Chinese application skills and key technical abilities in the vocational and technical fields, providing assistance for learners to quickly familiarize themselves with and adapt to the work environment. This series of textbooks is suitable for international employees engaged in relevant professions in Chinese companies, international students or trainees in China, as well as learners interested in Chinese language, culture, and vocational skills.

Livestock and Poultry Production Technology (Elementary) is one of the textbooks in the "Access to Vocational Chinese" series. It is suitable for international employees engaged in livestock and poultry production work in Chinese companies. Through studying this textbook, learners can achieve the goal of conducting simple work communication in Chinese, mastering skills ranging from safety regulations for new employees entering and exiting farms, to cleaning and disinfecting barns, and finally to basic operations for managing livestock and poultry.

The compilation of the textbook was based on the *Teaching Standards for Animal Husbandry and Veterinary Medicine*. Experts from the animal husbandry industry were consulted, and surveys were conducted with overseas Chinese-funded enterprises to understand their language, skills and overall quality requirements for employees. Real language materials from actual work scenarios and typical work tasks were reconstructed into texts and dialogues that meet the learners' level. The textbook consists of 30 lessons, each of which includes eight sections: review, warm-up, new vocabulary, text, grammar, writing, extension, and summary. It is richly illustrated with pictures to present real work scenarios in a visually engaging manner. In addition, audio, video and other resources have been developed to help learners acquire the ability to perform basic communication in Chinese within vocational contexts.

After studying this textbook, learners should be able to:

1. Develop basic ability to understand and use Chinese, laying a foundation for workplace application and advanced Chinese learning;
2. Master basic vocabulary, technical terms, and common expressions used in livestock and poultry production work, and apply them to daily communication and work exchanges;
3. Gain a basic knowledge of Chinese culture, recognize cultural differences when communicating with Chinese clients, and improve professional competitiveness.

This book has received great support from the Center for Language Education and Cooperation under the Ministry of Education, China Nonferrous Metal Industry Talent Center, and the expert panel, for which we would like to express our sincere gratitude. We also extend our thanks to Higher Education Press for their strong support and guidance.

The publication and application of the "Access to Vocational Chinese" series of textbooks aim to develop talents with "Chinese + Vocational Skills" across the globe, promote local economies, and make positive contributions to building a community with a shared future. Due to limited knowledge and related experience of the project team, as well as time constraints, this book is bound to have many deficiencies that need improvement. We sincerely invite users of this book to provide feedback on any issues discovered, so that we can make improvements in future editions and related materials.

Compiling team,

October 2024

目　录　Contents

第1课 Lesson 1

Rènshi tóngshì

认识同事 Meeting Colleagues

热身 Warming Up

看图选词。Look at the pictures and choose the correct words.

A 兽医 (shòuyī) veterinarian; vet	B 同事 (tóngshì) colleague; co-worker
C 高兴 (gāoxìng) happy; glad	D 饲养员 (sìyǎngyuán) animal keeper

1

2
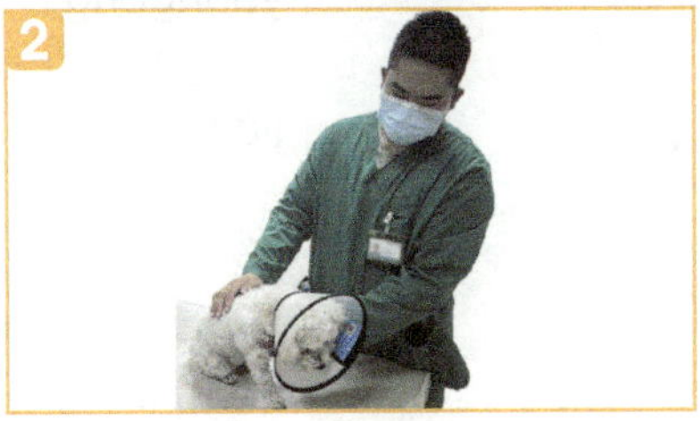

3

4

学习生词 Words and Expressions 1-1

1	认识	rènshi	*v.*	meet; know
2	同事	tóngshì	*n.*	colleague; co-worker
3	您	nín	*pron.*	you (*honorific*)
4	是	shì	*v.*	be verb
5	兽医	shòuyī	*n.*	veterinarian; vet
6	吗	ma	*aux.*	*modal particle*
7	我	wǒ	*pron.*	I; me
8	不	bù	*adv.*	no; not
9	饲养员	sìyǎngyuán		animal keeper
10	新	xīn	*adj.*	new
11	员工	yuángōng	*n.*	personnel; employee
12	叫	jiào	*v.*	be called
13	也	yě	*adv.*	also; too
14	很	hěn	*adv.*	very
15	高兴	gāoxìng	*adj.*	happy; glad

专有名词 Proper Nouns

16	大卫	Dàwèi	*proper noun*	David
17	王东	Wáng Dōng	*proper noun*	Wang Dong

词语练习 Words Exercises

1. 将中文词语和对应的拼音及英文连线。**Match the Chinese words with corresponding *pinyin* and English words.**

1 高兴	tóngshì	meet; know
2 认识	xīn	new
3 新	gāoxìng	colleague; co-worker
4 同事	rènshi	happy; glad

2. 词语分类。**Categorize the words.**

A 认识　B 同事　C 是　D 兽医　E 不　F 饲养员
G 新　H 员工　I 也　J 很　K 高兴

职业或身份的词语（words for professions or identities）：

____

学习课文 Text 1-2

Rènshi tóngshì
认识同事

Dàwèi: Nín shì shòuyī ma?
大卫：您是兽医吗？

Wáng Dōng: Wǒ bú shì shòuyī, wǒ shì sìyǎngyuán.
王　东：我不是兽医，我是饲养员。

Dàwèi : Nín shì xīn yuángōng ma?
大卫 ：您是新员工吗?

Wáng Dōng : Shì, wǒ shì xīn yuángōng.
王 东：是，我是新员工。

Dàwèi : Wǒ jiào Dàwèi, yě shì sìyǎngyuán.
大卫 ：我叫大卫，也是饲养员。

Wáng Dōng : Hěn gāoxìng rènshi nín.
王 东：很高兴认识您。

Dàwèi : Rènshi nín wǒ yě hěn gāoxìng.
大卫 ：认识您我也很高兴。

Meeting Colleagues

David: Are you a veterinarian?

Wang Dong: I am not a veterinarian. I am an animal keeper.

David: Are you a new employee?

Wang Dong: Yes, I am a new employee.

David: My name is David. I am an animal keeper, too.

Wang Dong: Nice to meet you.

David: Nice to meet you too.

课文练习 Text Exercises

1. 选词填空。Fill in the blanks with the correct words.

A 不　　B 吗　　C 新员工　　D 饲养员

1 大卫：您是兽医＿＿＿＿＿?

2 王东：我________是兽医，我是________。

3 大卫：您是________吗？

4 王东：是，我是新员工。

2. 判断正误。True or false.

1 王东是兽医。

2 王东不是饲养员。

3 王东是新员工。

4 大卫也是饲养员。

学习语法 Grammar

语法点 1 Grammar Point 1

语气助词：吗　Modal particle: 吗

用来放在陈述句句尾表示疑问，构成一般疑问句。回答一般用该陈述句的肯定形式（yes）或否定形式（no）。

It is used at the end of a declarative sentence to indicate a question, forming a general interrogative sentence. The response is generally given in the affirmative form (yes) or negative form (no) of the declarative sentence.

常用结构：主语 + 动词 + 宾语 + 吗？

Common structure: subject + verb + object + 吗？

例句：1 A：您是兽医吗？(Nín shì shòuyī ma?) Are you a veterinarian?

B：我是兽医。(Wǒ shì shòuyī.) I am a veterinarian.

Tā shì xīn yuángōng ma?
2 A：他是新员工吗？ Is he a new employee?
Tā bú shì xīn yuángōng.
B：他不是新员工。He is not a new employee.
Nǐ jiào Dàwèi ma?
3 A：你叫大卫吗？ Is your name David?
Wǒ jiào Dàwèi.
B：我叫大卫。My name is David.
Wǒ bú jiào Dàwèi.
我不叫大卫。My name is not David.

语法练习 1 Grammar Exercise 1

根据提示完成对话。Complete the conversations according to the prompts.

1 A：________________？
B：我是新员工。

2 A：________________？
B：我不是兽医。

3 A：你是饲养员吗？
B：________________。

4 A：你叫大卫吗？
B：________________。

语法点 2 Grammar Point 2

关联副词：也　Correlative adverb: 也

用来表示两个事物相同或类同，一般用在后一分句中。放在动词前面，如“也是”。与其他副词同时使用时一般放在其他副词前面，如“也不”。

It indicates the similarity or equivalence between two things and is typically used in the second clause of a sentence. It is placed before a verb, such as in “ 也是 ” (also; too). When used with other adverbs, it is generally placed before them, for instance, “ 也不 ” (neither; nor).

常用结构：主语 1 + 动词性短语，主语 2+ 也 + 动词性短语

Common structure: subject 1 + verb phrase, subject 2 + 也 + verb phrase

例句：

1. Dàwèi shì xīn yuángōng, Wáng Dōng yě shì xīn yuángōng.
大卫是新员工，王东也是新员工。David is a new employee, Wang Dong is also a new employee.

2. Dàwèi bú shì shòuyī, Wáng Dōng yě bú shì shòuyī.
大卫不是兽医，王东也不是兽医。David is not a veterinarian, and neither is Wang Dong.

3. Wǒ shì Zhōngguórén, tā yě shì Zhōngguórén.
我是中国人，他也是中国人。I am Chinese, and he is Chinese, too.

语法练习 2 Grammar Exercise 2

把“也”放在句中合适的位置。Put “也” in the right place of the sentence.

1. 大卫是饲养员，____王东____是____饲养员。
2. 他是新员工，____我____是____新员工。
3. 他是兽医，____我____是____兽医。
4. 大卫不是兽医，____王东____不____是兽医。

汉字书写 Writing Chinese Characters

yī 一

一	一	一	一	一						

èr 二

二	二	二	二	二						

sān 三

三	三	三	三	三						

sì 四 四 四 四 四

四	四	四	四	四						

职业拓展 Career Insight

High-Quality Development of Modern Animal Husbandry in China

In 2023, the Chinese government proposed to develop modern facility agriculture, implement upgrading actions to modernize facility agriculture, promote the transformation and upgrading of large-scale livestock and poultry farms as well as aquaculture ponds. China's livestock and poultry industry is gradually developing in the direction of large-scale, intensification and intelligence. Improved quality and efficiency is steadily achieved, making it a high-quality industry.

小结 Summary

词语 Words

朗读词语。**Read the words aloud.**

同事	兽医	新
饲养员	高兴	员工

语法 Grammar

语言点回顾。Language points review.

语言点	常用结构	例句
语气助词：吗	S + V + O + 吗？	您是兽医吗？ 他是新员工吗？
关联副词：也	S_1 + VP，S_2 + 也 + VP	王东是饲养员，我也是饲养员。 大卫不是兽医，王东也不是兽医。

课文理解 Text Comprehension

根据提示复述课文。Retell the text according to the prompts.

王东不是________，是饲养员，王东是________员工。大卫也是________。大卫很高兴________王东。

第2课 Lesson 2

Shúxi gōngzuò huánjìng

熟悉工作环境

Being Familiar with the Working Environment

复习 Revision

替换练习。Substitution drills.

例句：A：你是新员工吗？

B：我是 / 不是新员工。

A：你是 新员工 / 饲养员 / 兽医 / 王东 吗？

B：我 是 / 不是 新员工 / 饲养员 / 兽医 / 王东 。

热身 Warming Up

看图选词。**Look at the pictures and choose the correct words.**

A 物料间 (wùliàojiān) material room; storeroom	B 篮球场 (lánqiúchǎng) basketball court
C 生产区 (shēngchǎnqū) production area	D 食堂 (shítáng) canteen; dining hall

学习生词 Words and Expressions 2-1

1	熟悉	shúxi	*v.*	be familiar with
2	工作	gōngzuò	*n.*	working

3	环境	huánjìng	*n.*	environment
4	这	zhè	*pron.*	this
5	生产区	shēngchǎnqū		production area
6	物料间	wùliàojiān		material room; storeroom
7	在	zài	*v.*	be at / in / on (a place)
8	生活区	shēnghuóqū		living area
9	西边	xībian	*n.*	west side
10	宿舍楼	sùshèlóu		dormitory building
11	东边	dōngbian	*n.*	east side
12	办公楼	bàngōnglóu		office building
13	北边	běibian	*n.*	north side
14	食堂	shítáng	*n.*	cateen; dining hall
15	南边	nánbian	*n.*	south side
16	篮球场	lánqiúchǎng		basketball court

词语练习 Words Exercises

1. 词语分类。Categorize the words.

A 物料间　B 西边　C 宿舍楼　D 东边　E 办公楼
F 北边　G 食堂　H 南边　I 篮球场

1 方位名词（nouns of locality）：

____

2 场所（location）：

____

2. 选择正确的方位词。**Choose the proper nouns of locality.**

A 东边

B 西边

C 南边

D 北边

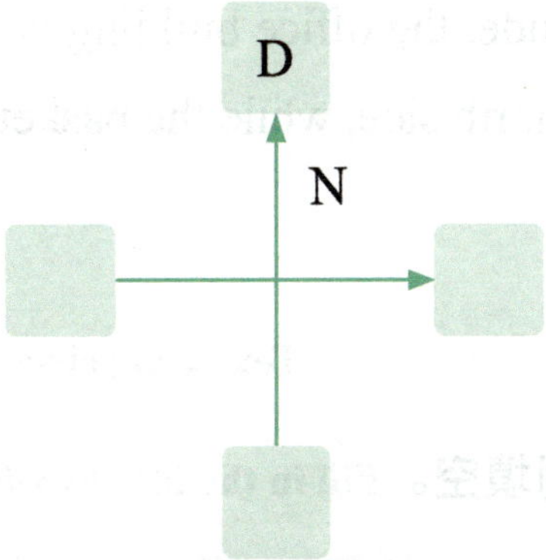

学习课文 Text 2-2

Shúxi gōngzuò huánjìng
熟悉工作环境

Zhè shì shēngchǎnqū, wùliàojiān zài shēngchǎnqū.
这是生产区，物料间在生产区。

Zhè shì shēnghuóqū: xībian shì sùshèlóu, dōngbian shì bàngōnglóu, běibian shì shítáng, nánbian shì lánqiúchǎng.
这是生活区：西边是宿舍楼，东边是办公楼，北边是食堂，南边是篮球场。

Being Familiar with the Working Environment

This is the production area. The material room is in the production area.

This is the living area, the dormitory building is on the west side, the office building is on the east side, the canteen is on the north side, while the basketball court is on the south side.

课文练习 Text Exercises

1. 选词填空。Fill in the blanks with the correct words.

A 生产区　　B 生活区

1. 物料间在________。
2. 宿舍楼在________。
3. 办公楼在________。
4. 食堂在________。

2. 判断正误。True or false.

1. 东边是宿舍楼。
2. 西边是办公楼。
3. 北边是食堂。
4. 南边是篮球场。

学习语法 Grammar

语法点 1 Grammar Point 1

特殊句型：“是”字句 Special sentence pattern: the 是 -sentence

表示存在，意思是什么地方有什么。

To indicate existence means to express that something exists in a certain place.

常用结构：主语（场所）+ 是 + 宾语

Common structure: subject (location) + 是 + object

例句：

1. Xībian shì sùshèlóu.
   西边是宿舍楼。The dormitory building is on the west side.
2. Dōngbian shì bàngōnglóu.
   东边是办公楼。The office building is on the east side.
3. Běibian shì shítáng.
   北边是食堂。The canteen is on the north side.

语法练习 1 Grammar Exercise 1

按照正确的语序连词成句。Make sentences in correct orders with the given words or phrases.

1. ①是 ②篮球场 ③南边

   ____

2. ①北边 ②办公楼 ③不是

   ____

3. ①宿舍楼 ②西边 ③是 ④吗

   ____

4 ①东边 ②生产区 ③是 ④不

____

语法点 2 Grammar Point 2

方位名词：东、西、南、北 Nouns of locality: 东 / 西 / 南 / 北

方位名词表示带有参照点的方向或相对位置，用在名词后面，表示处所。

Nouns of locality indicate directions or relative positions with reference points and are used after nouns to indicate locations.

常用结构：主语（某人 / 某物）+ 在 + 方位名词

Common structure: subject (sb / sth) + 在 + location noun

汉语表示方向的方位词主要有：

The nouns of locality in Chinese that mainly indicate directions include:

东	西	南	北
东边	西边	南边	北边

例句：
1. Sùshèlóu zài xībian.
宿舍楼在西边。The dormitory building is on the west side.
2. Bàngōnglóu zài dōngbian
办公楼在东边。The office building is on the east side.
3. Wǒ zài cāochǎng nánbian
我在操场南边。I am on the south side of the playground.

语法练习 2 Grammar Exercise 2

判断正误。True or false.

1. 办公楼在西边。
2. 篮球场在北边。
3. 食堂在南边。
4. 宿舍楼在东边。

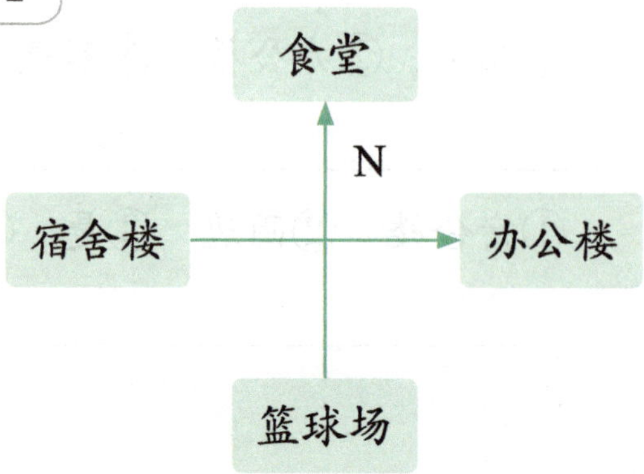

汉字书写 Writing Chinese Characters

wǔ 五 五 五 五

五 五 五 五 五

liù 六 六 六 六

六 六 六 六 六

qī 七 七

七 七 七 七 七

bā 八 八

八 八 八 八 八

文化拓展 Culture Insight

The Origin of the Name "China"

The origin of the name "China" is deeply rooted in geographical considerations. For instance, during the Shang Dynasty, the capital of the Shang Kingdom lay at the center of all vassal states to the east, south, west, and north, hence the land was known as "China", meaning the kingdom situated in the middle. Similarly, during the Zhou Dynasty, there was also the view that the capital established by the emperor was "China", which later evolved into a term referring to the habitation of the Huaxia ethnic group and the nation they established.

小结 Summary

词语 Words

选词填空。Fill in the blanks with the correct words.

A 东边	B 西边
C 南边	D 北边
E 食堂	F 办公楼
G 宿舍楼	H 篮球场

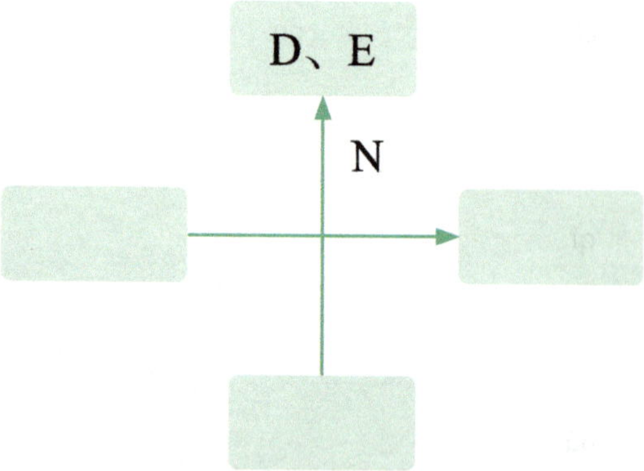

语法 Grammar

语言点回顾。Language points review.

语言点	常用结构	例句
特殊句型：“是”字句	S（location）+ 是 + O	西边是宿舍楼。 东边是办公楼。
方位名词：东、西、南、北	S（sb / sth）+ 在 + N方位	宿舍楼在西边。 我在操场南边。

课文理解 Text Comprehension

根据提示复述课文。Retell the text according to the prompts.

这是生产区，________在生产区。这是生活区：西边是________，东边是________，北边是________，南边是________。

第3课 Lesson 3

Cháng jiàn jiāqín

常见家禽 Common Poultry

复习 Revision

看图，参照例句说一说。Look at the picture and follow the example to speak sentences.

例句：西边是宿舍楼。

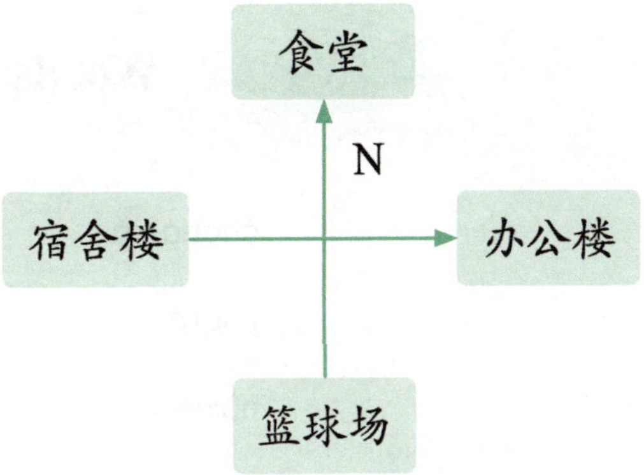

热身 Warming Up

看图选词。Look at the pictures and choose the correct words.

A 鸡(jī) chicken　B 鸭(yā) duck　C 鹅(é) goose　D 鸽子(gēzi) pigeon; dove

学习生词 Words and Expressions 3-1

1	常见	cháng jiàn		common
2	家禽	jiāqín	*n.*	poultry
3	哪些	nǎxiē	*pron.*	which
4	鸡	jī	*n.*	chicken
5	鸭	yā	*n.*	duck
6	鹅	é	*n.*	goose
7	鹌鹑	ānchun	*n.*	quail
8	它们	tāmen	*pron.*	they
9	鸽子	gēzi	*n.*	pigeon; dove
10	呢	ne	*aux.*	*modal particle*

专有名词 Proper Nouns

11	李山	Lǐ Shān	*proper noun*	Li Shan

词语练习 Words Exercises

1. 词语分类。**Categorize the words.**

A 鸡	B 物料间	C 鸭	D 鹅
E 篮球场	F 鹌鹑	G 食堂	H 鸽子

常见家禽（common poultry）：______________________

2. 将中文词语和对应的拼音及英文连线。**Match the Chinese words with corresponding *pinyin* and English words.**

1 鸡 •	• yā •	• chicken
2 鸭 •	• gēzi •	• goose
3 鹅 •	• jī •	• pigeon; dove
4 鸽子 •	• é •	• duck

学习课文 Text 3-2

Cháng jiàn jiāqín
常见家禽

Dàwèi : Nǎxiē shì cháng jiàn jiāqín?
大卫：哪些是常见家禽？

Lǐ Shān: jī, yā, é, ānchun, tāmen shì cháng jiàn jiāqín.
李山：鸡、鸭、鹅、鹌鹑，它们是常见家禽。

Dàwèi: Gēzi ne?
大卫：鸽子呢？

Lǐ Shān: Gēzi bú shì jiāqín.
李山：鸽子不是家禽。

Common Poultry

David: Which species of poultry are common?

Li Shan: Chicken, duck, goose and quail are common species of poultry.

David: What about pigeon?

Li Shan: Pigeon is not poultry.

课文练习 Text Exercises

1. 选词填空。Fill in the blanks with the correct words.

A 是　　B 哪些　　C 不是　　D 家禽

1. ________是常见家禽？
2. 鸡是常见________。
3. 鸽子________家禽。
4. 鸡、鸭、鹅、鹌鹑，它们________常见家禽。

2. 选择正确的答案。Choose the correct answers.

1 鸡是常见家禽吗？________

A 是　　B 不是

2 鸭是常见家禽，鹅呢？________

A 是　　B 不是

3 鹌鹑是常见家禽，鸽子呢？________

A 是　　B 不是

4 哪些是常见家禽？________

A 鸡　　B 鸭　　C 鸽子　　D 鹅　　E 鹌鹑

学习语法 Grammar

语法点 1 Grammar Point 1

疑问代词：哪些　Interrogative pronoun: 哪些

疑问代词“哪些”用在疑问句中，用来对多数的人或事物进行提问。可以放在主语、宾语或定语的位置上。

The interrogative pronoun “哪些” is used in interrogative sentences to inquire about a plurality of people or things. It can be placed in the position of subject, object, or attribute.

例句：

1 Nǎxiē shì chángjiàn jiāqín?
哪些是常见家禽？ Which are the common poultry?

2 Nǎxiē yuángōng shì sìyǎngyuán?
哪些员工是饲养员？ Which employees are the animal keepers?

3 Nǎxiē yuángōng shì xīn yuángōng?
哪些员工是新员工？ Which employees are new employees?

语法练习 1 Grammar Exercise 1

按照正确的语序连词成句。Make sentences in correct orders with the given words or phrases.

1 ①新员工 ②哪些 ③是

____

2 ①是 ②常见家禽 ③哪些

____

3 ①哪些 ②饲养员 ③是 ④员工

____

4 ①员工 ②哪些 ③新员工 ④是

____

语法点 2 Grammar Point 2

语气助词：呢　Modal particle：呢

可以用在省略疑问句中，疑问的内容根据上文来判断。

It can be used in ellipsis interrogative sentences, where the content of the question is determined based on the preceding context.

常用结构：……（A），B 呢？

Common structure：……（A），B 呢？

例句：

1 Jī shì chángjiàn jiāqín, gēzi ne? (Jī shì chángjiàn jiāqín, gēzi shì chángjiàn jiāqín ma?)
鸡是常见家禽，鸽子呢？（＝鸡是常见家禽，鸽子是常见家禽吗？）Chickens are common poultry, what about pigeons?

2 Wǒ shì xīn yuángōng, nǐ ne? (Wǒ shì xīn yuángōng, nǐ shì xīn yuángōng ma?)
我是新员工，你呢？（＝我是新员工，你是新员工吗？）I am a new employee, what about you?

3 Wǒ shì sìyǎngyuán, nǐ ne? (Wǒ shì sìyǎngyuán, nǐ shì sìyǎngyuán ma?)
我是饲养员，你呢？（=我是饲养员，你是饲养员吗？）I am an animal keeper, what about you?

语法练习 2 Grammar Exercise 2

用"呢"改写句子。Rewrite the sentences with "呢".

1 大卫是新员工，王东是新员工吗？

______________________________。

2 我是饲养员，你是饲养员吗？

______________________________。

3 鸡、鸭、鹅是家禽，鸽子是家禽吗？

______________________________。

4 食堂在生活区，办公楼在生活区吗？

______________________________。

汉字书写 Writing Chinese Characters

jiǔ 九 九

九 九 九 九 九

shí 十 十

十 十 十 十 十

bǎi 百 百 百 百 百 百

百 百 百 百 百

qiān 千 千 千

千 千 千 千 千

职业拓展 Career Insight

The Feeding and Behavioral Habits of Poultry

The feeding and behavioral habits of poultry vary from species to species. For instance, chickens prefer grains, insects, and earthworms, and they eat relatively quickly. On the other hand, geese are herbivores, good at consuming grass, straw, and other plant matter. Additionally, they are also good at consuming protein-rich feeds like bean cakes and bean residues. Understanding these habits is crucial in providing appropriate feed for poultry and ensuring their healthy growth.

小结 Summary

词语 Words

朗读词语。Read the words aloud.

常见	家禽	鸡	鸭
鹅	鹌鹑	鸽子	它们

语法 Grammar

语言点回顾。Language points review.

语言点	常用结构	例句
疑问代词：哪些	哪些 + VP？ 哪些 + N？	哪些是常见家禽？ 哪些员工是新员工？
语气助词：呢	……（A），B 呢？	鸡是常见家禽，鸽子呢？ 我是新员工，你呢？

课文理解 Text Comprehension

根据提示复述课文。Retell the text according to the prompts.

________、________、________、鹌鹑，它们是常见________，鸽子________家禽。

第4课 Lesson 4

Cháng jiàn jiāchù
常见家畜
Common Livestock

复习 Revision

判断正误。True or false.

1 鸡是常见家禽。

2 鸽子是常见家禽。

3 鹅是家禽。

4 鹌鹑不是家禽。

热身 Warming Up

看图选词。Look at the pictures and choose the correct words.

A 猪 (zhū) pig	B 牛 (niú) cattle
C 羊 (yáng) sheep	D 养殖场 (yǎngzhíchǎng) livestock and poultry farm

1

2

3

4

学习生词 Words and Expressions 4-1

1	家畜	jiāchù	*n.*	livestock
2	我们	wǒmen	*pron.*	we; us
3	公司	gōngsī	*n.*	company
4	有	yǒu	*v.*	have
5	几	jǐ	*num.*	how many
6	个	gè	*measure word*	*measure word*
7	养殖场	yǎngzhíchǎng		livestock and poultry farm
8	三	sān	*num.*	three

9	养	yǎng	*v.*	raise; keep
10	牛	niú	*n.*	cattle
11	羊	yáng	*n.*	sheep
12	和	hé	*conj.*	and
13	猪	zhū	*n.*	pig

词语练习 Words Exercises

1. 将中文词语和对应的拼音及英文连线。Match the Chinese words with corresponding *pinyin* and English words.

1 家畜	niú	cattle
2 牛	jiāchù	livestock
3 羊	zhū	pig
4 猪	yáng	sheep

2. 词语分类。Categorize the words.

A 鸡	B 牛	C 鸭	D 鹅
E 羊	F 鹌鹑	G 猪	H 鸽子

常见家畜（common livestock）：

____

学习课文 Text 4-2

Cháng jiàn jiāchù
常见家畜

Dàwèi : Wǒmen gōngsī yǒu jǐ ge yǎngzhíchǎng?
大卫：我们公司有几个养殖场？

Lǐ Shān : Wǒmen gōngsī yǒu sān ge yǎngzhíchǎng.
李山：我们公司有三个养殖场。

Dàwèi : Yǎng nǎxiē jiāchù ne?
大卫：养哪些家畜呢？

Lǐ Shān : Yǎng niú, yáng hé zhū.
李山：养牛、羊和猪。

Common Livestock

David: How many livestock and poultry farms does our company have?

Li Shan: Our company has three livestock and poultry farms.

David: What kinds of livestock do we raise?

Li Shan: We raise cattle, sheep and pigs.

课文练习 Text Exercises

1. 选词填空。Fill in the blanks with the correct words.

A 个　　B 哪些　　C 几　　D 养

1. 我们公司有________个养殖场？
2. 我们公司有三________养殖场。
3. 养________家畜呢？
4. 我们公司________牛、羊和猪。

2. 判断正误。True or false.

1. 我们公司有一个养殖场。
2. 牛是家畜。
3. 猪是家畜。
4. 羊不是家畜。

学习语法 Grammar

语法点 1 Grammar Point 1

名量词：个、只、头　Nominal measure words: 个 / 只 / 头

量词表示计量单位，汉语的数词和名词之间一般要用量词。名量词用来表示事物数量的量词，它们通常与名词一起使用，用于指明数量或计量单位。“个”可以用于人，也可以用于东西，如“一个人、三个养殖场”。“只”用于计量动物或某些成对东西中的一个，如“一只鸡、两只羊、两只手”。“头”用于计量体型较大的动物，如“一头牛”。

Measure word represents a unit of measurement. In Chinese, it is usually used between a number and a noun. Nominal measure word is used to express the quantity of objects, and it is typically used together with nouns to specify the amount or measurement unit. “个” can be used for people or things, such as “一个人 (one person), 三个养殖场 (three livestock and poultry farms)”. “只” is used to measure an animal or one of certain pairs of things, such as “一只鸡 (a chicken), 三只羊 (three sheep), 一只手 (one hand)”. “头” is used to measure larger animals, such as “一头牛 (a head of cattle)”.

常用结构：数词 + 量词 + 名词

Common structure: numeral + measure word + noun

例：

shùcí 数词	liàngcí 量词	míngcí 名词
sān 三	gè 个	yǎngzhíchǎng 养殖场
yī 一	zhī 只	jī 鸡
yī 一	zhī 只	shǒu 手
yī 一	tóu 头	niú 牛

语法练习 1 Grammar Exercise 1

选词填空。Fill in the blanks with the correct words.

A 个　　B 只　　C 头

1 我们公司有三________养殖场。

2 养殖场有60________牛。

3 养殖场有500________鸡。

4 公司有三________新员工。

语法点 2 Grammar Point 2

疑问代词：几　Interrogative pronoun: 几

“几”用在疑问句中表示询问数量。一般用来询问“10”以下或说话人认为很少的数量，多用于口语。后面要带量词。

“几”is used in interrogative sentences to ask about quantity. The number referred to is typically smaller than “10” or considered to be very small. It is usually used in spoken Chinese.

常用结构：主语 + 动词 + 几 + 量词 + 名词？

Common structure: subject + verb + 几 + measure word + noun ?

例句：

1 Wǒmen gōngsī yǒu jǐ ge yǎngzhíchǎng?
我们公司有几个养殖场？ How many livestock and poultry farms does our company have?

2 Wǒmen yǎngzhíchǎng yǒu jǐ ge sìyǎngyuán?
我们养殖场有几个饲养员？ How many animal keepers does our livestock farm have?

3 Rén yǒu jǐ zhī shǒu?
人有几只手？ How many hands does a person have?

语法练习 2 Grammar Exercise 2

按照正确的语序连词成句。Make sentences in correct orders with the given words or phrases.

1 ①几　②养殖场　③个　④我们公司　⑤有

____

2 ①个 ②几 ③我们公司 ④食堂 ⑤有

3 ①新员工 ②个 ③几 ④有 ⑤养殖场

4 ①篮球场 ②个 ③几 ④有 ⑤人

汉字书写 Writing Chinese Characters

wàn 万万万

万 万 万 万 万

yì 亿亿亿

亿 亿 亿 亿 亿

nǐ 你你你你你你你

你 你 你 你 你

tā 他他他他他

他 他 他 他 他

文化拓展 Culture Insight

The Six Domestic Animals Thrive

The Chinese idiom "The six domestic animals thrive" originated from ancient Chinese literature, refers to the prosperity of various livestock and poultry. This idiom not only describes the flourishing of domestic animal reproduction, but it is also often used as a symbol of agricultural prosperity and affluent life. The term "six domestic animals" usually includes horses, cattle, sheep, pigs, dogs and chickens. Each type of domestic animal has its specific function and significance, such as horses being able to carry heavy loads and travel long distances, cattle being able to till the land, sheep being able to provide sacrificial vessels, pigs being able to provide meat, dogs being able to guard against dangers at night, chickens being able to crow at dawn. In terms of cultural connotation, the six domestic animals also represent the deep relationship between people and animals, reflecting the development of human society and the progress of civilization.

小结 Summary

词语 Words

词语搭配连线。**Match the words.**

	• 只 •	• 牛
一 •	• 个 •	• 鸡
	• 头 •	• 人

语法 Grammar

语言点回顾。Language points review.

语言点	常用结构	例句
名量词：个、只、头	Num + M + N	三个养殖场。 一只鸡。
疑问代词：几	S + V + 几 + M + N？	我们公司有几个养殖场？ 我们养殖场有几个饲养员？

课文理解 Text Comprehension

根据提示复述课文。Retell the text according to the prompts.

我们公司有三________养殖场，养________、________和________。

第5课 Lesson 5

Jìnrù yǎngzhíchǎng

进入养殖场

Entering the Livestock and Poultry Farm

复习 Revision

根据提示练习说句子。**Practice speaking sentences according to the prompts.**

我们公司有三个养殖场。一个养________，一个养________，一个养________。

热身 Warming Up

看图选词。**Look at the pictures and choose the correct words.**

A 紫外线灯 (zǐwàixiàndēng) UV lamps	B 工作服 (gōngzuòfú) working clothes
C 工作鞋 (gōngzuòxié) working shoes	D 消毒液 (xiāodúyè) disinfectant

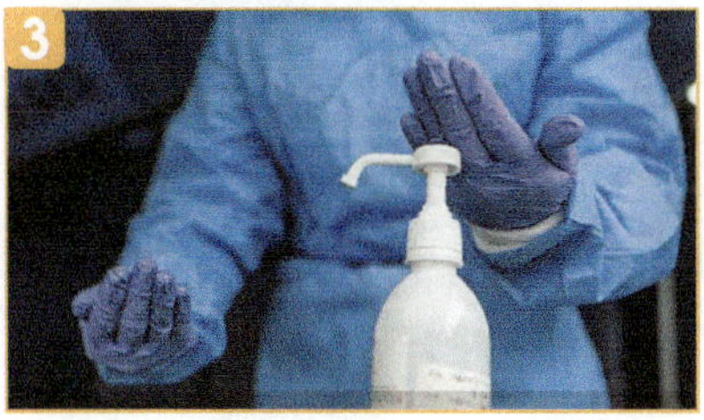

学习生词 Words and Expressions 5-1

1	进入	jìnrù	*v.*	enter
2	洗澡间	xǐzǎojiān		bath room
3	洗澡	xǐzǎo	*v.*	take a bath
4	更衣室	gēngyīshì	*n.*	locker room
5	穿	chuān	*v.*	dress; wear; put on
6	工作服	gōngzuòfú	*n.*	working clothes
7	工作鞋	gōngzuòxié		working shoes

8	用	yòng	v.	use
9	消毒液	xiāodúyè		disinfectant
10	擦拭	cāshì	v.	wipe
11	随身	suíshēn	adj.	carry-on; personal
12	物品	wùpǐn	n.	article; goods
13	紫外线灯	zǐwàixiàndēng		UV lamp
14	消毒	xiāodú	v.	disinfect

词语练习 Words Exercises

1. 词语搭配连线。Match the words.

1 穿 •	• 工作服
	• 洗澡间
2 进入 •	• 更衣室
	• 工作鞋

2. 将中文词语和对应的拼音及英文连线。Match the Chinese words with corresponding *pinyin* and English words.

1 进入 •	• yòng •	• use
2 穿 •	• jìnrù •	• enter
3 用 •	• cāshì •	• wipe
4 擦拭 •	• chuān •	• dress; wear; put on

学习课文 Text 5-2

Jìnrù yǎngzhíchǎng
进入养殖场

Jìnrù xǐzǎojiān xǐzǎo.
1. 进入洗澡间洗澡。

Jìnrù gēngyīshì chuān gōngzuòfú hé gōngzuòxié.
2. 进入更衣室穿工作服和工作鞋。

Yòng xiāodúyè cāshì suíshēn wùpǐn, yòng zǐwàixiàndēng xiāodú.
3. 用消毒液擦拭随身物品，用紫外线灯消毒。

Jìnrù yǎngzhíchǎng.
4. 进入养殖场。

Entering the Livestock and Poultry Farm

1. Enter the bathroom to take a shower.

2. Enter the locker room to put on working clothes and working shoes.

3. Wipe personal belongings with disinfectant and disinfect them with UV lamps.

4. Enter the livestock and poultry farm.

课文练习 Text Exercises

1. 选词填空。Fill in the blanks with the correct words.

A 穿　　B 擦拭　　C 消毒　　D 洗澡

1. 进入洗澡间________。
2. 进入更衣室________工作服和工作鞋。
3. 用消毒液________随身物品。
4. 用紫外线灯________。

2. 根据课文内容给下列说法排序。Put the statements in the correct order according to the text.

1. 进入更衣室穿工作服和工作鞋。
2. 进入养殖场。
3. 用消毒液擦拭随身物品，用紫外线灯消毒。
4. 进入洗澡间洗澡。

____

学习语法 Grammar

语法点 1 Grammar Point 1

特殊句型：连动句（1） Special sentence pattern: sentence with a serial verb construction (1)

由同一个主语发出的两个或两个以上的动作的句子是连动句。一种连动句中，前一动作是后一动作的方式。

It is a sentence whose predicate consists of two or more verbs or verb phrases, indicating the subject performs two or more actions in sequences. One action follows the other , with the former being the manner of the latter.

常用结构：主语 + 动词性短语 1（表方式）+ 动词性短语 2

Common structure: subject + verb phrase 1 (manner) + verb phrase 2

例句：1 Wǒ yòng xiāodúyè cāshì suíshēn wùpǐn.
我用消毒液擦拭随身物品。I wipe my belongings with disinfectant.

2 Qǐng yòng zǐwàixiàndēng xiāodú gōngzuòfú.
请用紫外线灯消毒工作服。Please disinfect the working clothes with UV lamps.

3 Wǒ yòng zǐwàixiàndēng xiāodú gōngzuòxié.
我用紫外线灯消毒工作鞋。I disinfect the working shoes with UV lamps.

语法练习 1 Grammar Exercise 1

按照正确的语序连词成句。Make sentences in correct orders with the given words or phrases.

1 ①消毒工作服 ②用 ③紫外线灯

我______________________________。

2 ①用 ②消毒液 ③消毒工作鞋

员工______________________________。

3 ①消毒液 ②用 ③消毒 ④工作服

我______________________________。

4 ①用 ②紫外线灯 ③消毒 ④随身物品

我______________________________。

语法点 2 Grammar Point 2

特殊句型：连动句（2） Special sentence pattern: sentence with a serial verb construction (2)

两个或两个以上的动作由同一个主语发出的句子是连动句。一种连动句中，后一动作是前一动作的目的。

It is a sentence whose predicate consists of two or more verbs or verb phrases, indicating the subject performs two or more actions in sequences. One action follows the other , with the latter being the purpose of the former.

常用结构：主语＋动词性短语 1+ 动词性短语 2（表目的）

Common structure: subject + verb phrase 1 + verb phrase 2 (purpose)

例句：

1. Jìnrù xǐzǎojiān xǐzǎo.
   进入洗澡间洗澡。Enter the bathroom to take a shower.
2. Wǒ jìnrù gēngyīshì chuān gōngzuòfú.
   我进入更衣室穿工作服。I enter the locker room to put on working clothes.
3. Dàwèi lái Zhōngguó xuéxí Hànyǔ.
   大卫来中国学习汉语。David come to China to study Chinese.

语法练习 2 Grammar Exercise 2

按照正确的语序连词成句。Make sentences in correct orders with the given words or phrases.

1. ①穿工作服 ②进入更衣室

   我________________________________。

2. ①进入洗澡间 ②洗澡

   大卫________________________________。

3. ①穿工作鞋 ②进入更衣室

   我________________________________。

4 ①学习汉语 ②来中国

大卫________________________________。

汉字书写 Writing Chinese Characters

tǔ 土 土 土

土	土	土	土	土						

wáng 王 王 王 王

王	王	王	王	王						

yù 玉 玉 玉 玉 玉

玉	玉	玉	玉	玉						

zhǔ 主 主 主 主 主

主	主	主	主	主						

职业拓展 Career Insight

Employee Entry Requirements

Strengthen epidemic prevention at the farm entrance guard. There is disinfectant in the disinfection tank at the entrance of the livestock and poultry farm or production area. The disinfection room is equipped with UV lamps. Non-authorized personnel are not allowed to enter the production area without permission. Entrants must first change into special working clothes, caps and shoes, and can enter the livestock and poultry farm only after disinfection and sterilization in the disinfection tank and disinfection room.

小结 Summary

词语 Words

朗读词语。Read the words aloud.

进入	洗澡间	洗澡	更衣室	穿
工作服	工作鞋	用	消毒液	擦拭
随身物品		紫外线灯		消毒

语法 Grammar

语言点回顾。Language points review.

语言点	常用结构	例句
连动句：动词性短语1表方式	S+VP_1（表方式）+VP_2	我用消毒液擦拭随身物品。 我用紫外线灯消毒工作服。
连动句：动词性短语2表目的	S+VP_1+VP_2（表目的）	我进入洗澡间洗澡。 我进入更衣室穿工作服。

课文理解 Text Comprehension

根据提示复述课文。Retell the text according to the prompts.

1 进入________洗澡。

2 进入更衣室穿________和________。

3 用________擦拭随身物品，用________消毒。

4 进入养殖场。

第6课 Lesson 6

Chū yǎngzhíchǎng
出养殖场
Exiting the Livestock and Poultry Farm

复习 Revision

朗读句子。**Read the sentences aloud.**

1 进入洗澡间洗澡。

2 进入更衣室穿工作服和工作鞋。

3 用消毒液擦拭随身物品。

4 用紫外线灯消毒。

热身 Warming Up

看图选词。**Look at the pictures and choose the correct words.**

A 手机 (shǒujī) mobile phone	B 衣服 (yīfu) clothes
C 耳机 (ěrjī) earphone	D 眼镜 (yǎnjìng) glasses

1

2

3

4

学习生词 Words and Expressions 6-1

1	出	chū	*v.*	exit
2	内	nèi	*n.*	inside
3	脱下	tuōxià		take off
4	外	wài	*n.*	outside
5	衣服	yīfu	*n.*	clothes
6	手机	shǒujī	*n.*	mobile phone
7	耳机	ěrjī	*n.*	earphone
8	眼镜	yǎnjìng	*n.*	glasses
9	等	děng	*aux.*	and so on

词语练习 Words Exercises

1. 将中文词语和对应的拼音及英文连线。Match the Chinese words with corresponding *pinyin* and English words.

1 脱下	chū	exit
2 穿	tuōxià	and so on
3 出	děng	put on
4 等	chuān	take off

2. 词语分类。Categorize the words.

A 篮球场　B 物料间　C 手机　D 紫外线灯
E 耳机　F 家畜　G 眼镜

随身物品的词语（words for personal belongings）：

____

学习课文 Text 6-2

Chū yǎngzhíchǎng
出养殖场

zài nèi gēngyīshì tuōxia gōngzuòfú.
1. 在内更衣室脱下工作服。

Jìnrù xǐzǎojiān xǐzǎo.
2. 进入洗澡间洗澡。

Jìnrù wài gēngyīshì chuān yīfu.
3. 进入外更衣室穿衣服。

shǒujī, ěrjī, yǎnjìng děng suíshēn wùpǐn yòng xiāodúyè cāshì, yòng zǐwàixiàndēng xiāodú.
4. 手机、耳机、眼镜等随身物品用消毒液擦拭、用紫外线灯消毒。

Chū yǎngzhíchǎng.
5. 出养殖场。

Exiting the Livestock and Poultry Farm

1. Take off working clothes in the inner locker room.
2. Take a shower in the bathroom.
3. Enter the outer locker room to put on clothes.
4. Mobile phones, earphones, glasses, and other personal belongings should be wiped with disinfectant and disinfected with UV lamps.
5. Exit the livestock and poultry farm.

课文练习 Text Exercises

1. 选词填空。Fill in the blanks with the correct words.

A 紫外线灯　B 内更衣室　C 外更衣室　D 洗澡　E 消毒液

1 在________脱下工作服。

2 进入洗澡间________。

3 进入________穿衣服。

4 手机、耳机、眼镜等随身物品用________擦拭，用________消毒。

2. 根据课文内容给下列说法排序。Put the statements in the correct order according to the text.

1 进入外更衣室穿衣服。

2 在内更衣室脱下工作服。

3 进入洗澡间洗澡。

4 手机、耳机、眼镜等随身物品用消毒液擦拭、用紫外线灯消毒。

5 出养殖场。

____

学习语法 Grammar

语法点 1 Grammar Point 1

介词：在　Preposition: 在

介词“在”和后面的名词或名词性短语组成介词结构，表示动作行为进行的处所、范围或事物存在的位置。汉语的介词结构一般放在动词的前面做状语。

The preposition “在” combined with location nouns behind it forms a prepositional structure, indicating the location, scope, or position where an action or behavior takes place. In Chinese, the prepositional structure is usually placed in front of the verb as an adverbial.

常用结构：主语 + 在 + 处所 + 动词性短语

Common structure: subject + 在 + location + verb phrase

例句：1 Wǒ zài nèi gēngyīshì tuōxia gōngzuòfú.
我在内更衣室脱下工作服。I take off working clothes in the inner locker room.

2 Wǒ zài shítáng chīfàn.
我在食堂吃饭。I have a meal in the canteen.

3 Dàwèi zài xǐzǎojiān xǐzǎo.
大卫在洗澡间洗澡。David takes a shower in the bathroom.

语法练习 1 Grammar Exercise 1

替换练习。**Substitution drills.**

例句：我在内更衣室脱下工作服。

我 员工 他们	在	内更衣室 洗澡间 外更衣室 食堂	脱下工作服。 洗澡。 穿衣服。 吃饭。

语法点 2 Grammar Point 2

其他助词：等　Other particle: 等

助词“等”用在表示列举的多项词语后边，表示列举未尽，有省略或替代未列举部分的作用。

The auxiliary word “等” is used after a list of items to indicate that the enumeration is incomplete, suggesting the presence of omitted or substituted items.

常用结构：……A、B（、C……）+ 等

Common structure: ……A、B (、C……) + 等

例句：

1 Yǎngzhíchǎng li yǒu jī, yā, é děng.
养殖场里有鸡、鸭、鹅等。There are chickens, ducks, geese, and so on in the livestock and poultry farm.

2 Yǎngzhíchǎng li yǒu zhū, niú, yáng děng jiāchù.
养殖场里有猪、牛、羊等家畜。There are pigs, cattle, sheep, and so on in the livestock and poultry farm.

3 Yòng zǐwàixiàn xiāodú shǒujī, ěrjī, yǎnjìng děng suíshēn wùpǐn.
用紫外线消毒手机、耳机、眼镜等随身物品。Mobile phones, earphones, glasses, and other personal belongings should be disinfected with UV lamps.

语法练习 2 Grammar Exercise 2

把“等”放在句中合适的位置。Put “ 等 ” in the right place of the sentence.

1 养殖场里有鸡、鸭、____鹅____。

2 养殖场里有猪、牛、羊____家畜____。

3 用紫外线消毒手机、耳机、眼镜____随身物品____。

4 大卫、王东、李山____是饲养员____。

汉字书写 Writing Chinese Characters

rén 人 人

人 人 人 人 人

gè 个 个 个

个 个 个 个 个

cóng 从 从 从 从

从 从 从 从 从

zhòng 众众众众众众

众	众	众	众	众						

文化拓展 Culture Insight

Mending the Sky and Bathing the Sun

Ancient Chinese myths depict Nüwa mending the sky with five-colored stones and Xihe bathing the sun. These stories illustrate the magnificent achievements of great deeds, symbolizing the Chinese people's ability to overcome difficulties through their wisdom, pioneering spirit and unwavering perseverance, ultimately achieving harmony between humanity and nature. And the Chinese people have accomplished remarkable feats, such as the Red Flag Canal, sand control project, and the Three Gorges Dam, creating one after another miracles of achieving harmony between humanity and nature.

小结 Summary

词语 Words

朗读词语。Read the words aloud.

出	内	脱下	外
衣服	手机	耳机	眼镜

语法 Grammar

语言点回顾。**Language points review.**

语言点	常用结构	例句
介词：在	S + 在 + L + VP	员工在内更衣室脱下工作服。 我在食堂吃饭。
其他助词：等	……A、B （、C……）+ 等	手机、耳机、眼镜等随身物品用消毒液擦拭。 养殖场里有鸡、鸭、鹅等。

课文理解 Text Comprehension

根据提示复述课文。**Retell the text according to the prompts.**

1. 在________脱下工作服。
2. 进入________洗澡。
3. 进入________穿衣服。
4. 手机、耳机、眼镜________随身物品用消毒液________、用紫外线灯________。
5. 出养殖场。

第7课 Lesson 7

Zhěnglǐ juànshè
整理圈舍
Tidying up Animal Pens

复习 Revision

朗读句子。Read the sentences aloud.

1. 在内更衣室脱下工作服。
2. 进入洗澡间洗澡。
3. 进入外更衣室穿衣服。
4. 手机、耳机、眼镜等随身物品用消毒液擦拭、用紫外线灯消毒。

热身 Warming Up

看图选词。Look at the pictures and choose the correct words.

A 插座 (chāzuò) socket	B 补料槽 (bǔliàocáo) supplemental feeding trough
C 保护罩 (bǎohùzhào) protection cover	D 保温灯 (bǎowēndēng) heat lamp

1

2

3

4

学习生词 Words and Expressions 7-1

1	整理	zhěnglǐ	v.	tidy up
2	圈舍	juànshè		animal pen
3	先……，然后……（最后……）	xiān..., ránhòu... (zuìhòu...)		Firstly..., then... (finally...)
4	要	yào	v.	must; should
5	清理	qīnglǐ	v.	clean away
6	垃圾	lājī	n.	rubbish
7	移走	yízǒu		remove

8	保温灯	bǎowēndēng		heat lamp
9	补料槽	bǔliàocáo		supplemental feeding trough
10	设备	shèbèi	*n.*	equipment
11	放入	fàngrù		put into
12	关闭	guānbì	*v.*	turn off
13	电源	diànyuán	*n.*	power
14	插座	chāzuò	*n.*	socket
15	保护罩	bǎohùzhào		protection cover

词语练习 Words Exercises

1. 将中文词语和对应的拼音及英文连线。Match the Chinese words with corresponding *pinyin* and English words.

1 圈舍	yízǒu	remove
2 整理	juànshè	tidy up
3 清理	zhěnglǐ	animal pen
4 移走	qīnglǐ	clean away

2. 词语搭配连线。Match the words.

1 移走	设备
	电源
	补料槽
2 关闭	插座保护罩

学习课文 Text 7-2

Zhěnglǐ juànshè
整理圈舍

Zhěnglǐ juànshè, xiān yào qīnglǐ lājī.
整理圈舍，先要清理垃圾。

Ránhòu yízǒu bǎowēndēng, bǔliàocáo děng shèbèi, yòng xiāodúyè cāshì xiāodú, fàngrù wùliàojiān.
然后移走保温灯、补料槽等设备，用消毒液擦拭消毒，放入物料间。

Zuìhòu yào guānbì diànyuán hé chāzuò bǎohùzhào.
最后要关闭电源和插座保护罩。

Tidying up Animal Pens

When tidying up animal pens, we should clear away rubbish first. Then remove equipment like heat lamps and supplemental feeding troughs. Wipe and disinfect them with disinfectant, then put them into the material room. Finally, turn off the power and close the socket protection cover.

课文练习 Text Exercises

1. 选词填空。Fill in the blanks with the correct words.

A 保温灯和补料槽等设备	B 清理
C 电源和插座保护罩	D 物料间

1 首先________垃圾。
2 然后移走________。
3 用消毒液擦拭消毒，放入________。
4 最后要关闭________。

2. 根据课文内容给下列说法排序。Put the statements in the correct order according to the text.

1 最后要关闭电源，关闭插座保护罩。
2 先清理垃圾。
3 用消毒液擦拭保温灯、补料槽等设备，放入物料间。
4 然后移走保温灯、补料槽等设备。

____

学习语法 Grammar

语法点 1 Grammar Point 1

承接复句：先……，然后……（最后……） Successive complex sentence: 先……，然后……（最后……）

表示承接关系的复句，由三个分句组成，每个分句的顺序不能颠倒。

A complex sentence expressing a consecutive relationship and consists of three clauses, and the order of each clause cannot be reversed.

常用结构：主语 + 先 + 谓语 1，然后 + 谓语 2（，最后 + 谓语 3）

Common structure: subject + 先 + predicate 1, 然后 + predicate 2 (, 最后 + predicate 3)

例句：1 Wǒmen xiān qīnglǐ lājī, ránhòu yízǒu bǎowēndēng, bǔliàocáo děng shèbèi, zuìhòu guānbì diànyuán.
我们先清理垃圾，然后移走保温灯、补料槽等设备，最后关闭电源。We should first clear away rubbish, then remove equipment such as heat lamps and supplemental feeding troughs, and finally turn off the power.

2 (Jìnrù yǎngzhíchǎng) Wǒmen xiān jìnrù xǐzǎojiān xǐzǎo, ránhòu jìnrù gēngyīshì chuān gōngzuòfú hé gōngzuòxié, zuìhòu yòng xiāodúyè cāshì suíshēn wùpǐn.
（进入养殖场）我们先进入洗澡间洗澡，然后进入更衣室穿工作服和工作鞋，最后用消毒液擦拭随身物品。(Entering the livestock and poultry farm) We first enter the bathroom to take a shower, then enter the locker room to put on working clothes and working shoes, and finally wipe personal belongings with disinfectant.

3 Wǒmen xiān dú shēngcí, ránhòu dú kèwén, zuìhòu zuò liànxí.
我们先读生词，然后读课文，最后做练习。We read the new words first, then read the text, and finally do the exercises.

语法练习 1 Grammar Exercise 1

替换练习。Substitution drills.

例句：我先清理垃圾，然后移走设备，最后关闭电源。

我	清理垃圾	移走设备	关闭电源。
	洗澡	穿工作服	消毒随身物品。
	脱下工作服	洗澡	穿衣服。
	用消毒液擦拭	用紫外线消毒	出养殖场。

语法点 2 Grammar Point 2

能愿动词：要　Modal verb: 要

能愿动词是表示可能、必要、必然、意愿、估计等意义的一类动词，后面紧跟动词。能愿动词“要”表示应该、必须。

Modal verbs are a kind of verbs that indicate possibility, necessity, inevitability, willingness, and estimation, etc. They are followed by verbs. Modal verb “要” means should or must.

常用结构：主语 + 要 + 动词性短语

Common structure: subject + 要 + verb phrase

例句：

1. Zuìhòu yào guānbì diànyuán hé chāzuò bǎohùzhào.
最后要关闭电源和插座保护罩。Finally, turn off the power and close the socket protection cover.

2. Wǒmen yào yòng xiāodúyè cāshì suíshēn wùpǐn.
我们要用消毒液擦拭随身物品。We should wipe our belongings with disinfectant.

3. Wǒmen yào zài nèi gēngyīshì tuōxia gōngzuòfú.
我们要在内更衣室脱下工作服。We should take off our work clothes in the inner locker room.

语法练习 2 Grammar Exercise 2

按照正确的语序连词成句。Make sentences in correct orders with the given words or phrases.

1. ①电源　②关闭　③要　④我们

____

2. ①要　②穿　③我们　④工作服

____

3. ①消毒液　②用　③要　④我们　⑤随身物品　⑥擦拭

____

4 ①内更衣室 ②我们 ③要 ④在 ⑤工作服 ⑥脱下

____

汉字书写 Writing Chinese Characters

kǒu 口 口 口

口	口	口	口	口						

rì 日 日 日 日

日	日	日	日	日						

mù 目 目 目 目 目

目	目	目	目	目						

tián 田 田 田 田 田

田	田	田	田	田						

职业拓展 Career Insight

How to Keep Animal Pens Clean?

Animal pens should provide a good environment for animals in order to achieve greater economic benefits. Feed animals according to their sizes, and clean animal pens daily, perform regular comprehensive disinfection, ventilate and timely eradicate mosquitoes and flies.

小结 Summary

词语 Words

朗读词语。Read the words aloud.

整理	圈舍	清理	垃圾	移走
保温灯	补料槽	设备	放入	关闭
电源	插座	保护罩		

语法 Grammar

语言点回顾。Language points review.

语言点	常用结构	例句
承接复句：先……，然后……（最后……）	S + 先 + P_1，然后 + P_2（，最后 + P_3）	我们先清理垃圾，然后移走保温灯、补料槽等设备，最后关闭电源。 先脱下工作服，然后洗澡，最后用紫外线灯消毒。
能愿动词：要	S + 要 + VP	我们要用消毒液擦拭随身物品。 员工最后要关闭电源。

课文理解 Text Comprehension

根据提示复述课文。Retell the text according to the prompts.

整理圈舍，先要________垃圾。然后移走________、________等设备。用消毒液擦拭________，放入________。最后要关闭________和________。

第8课 Lesson 8

Qīngsǎo juànshè
清扫圈舍
Sweeping Animal Pens

复习 Revision

朗读句子。Read the sentences aloud.

1 整理圈舍，先要清理垃圾。

2 然后移走保温灯、补料槽等设备，用消毒液擦拭消毒，放入物料间。

3 最后要关闭电源和插座保护罩。

热身 Warming Up

看图选词。Look at the pictures and choose the correct words.

A 铁铲 (tiěchǎn) shovel	B 围栏 (wéilán) fence
C 地板 (dìbǎn) floor	D 扫帚 (sàozhou) broom

1

2

3
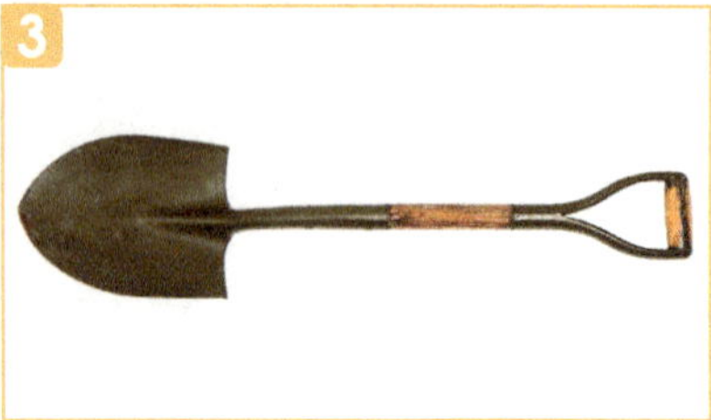

4

学习生词 Words and Expressions 8-1

1	清扫	qīngsǎo	*v.*	sweep
2	扫帚	sàozhou	*n.*	broom
3	地板	dìbǎn	*n.*	floor
4	料槽	liàocáo		feeding trough
5	围栏	wéilán		fence
6	铁铲	tiěchǎn		shovel
7	污物	wūwù	*n.*	dirt
8	难	nán	*adj.*	hard
9	的	de	*aux.*	*structural particle*
10	可以	kěyǐ	*v.*	can; may

11	洒	sǎ	*v.*	spray
12	水	shuǐ	*n.*	water
13	浸泡	jìnpào	*v.*	soak

词语练习 Words Exercises

1. 将中文词语和对应的拼音及英文连线。Match the Chinese words with corresponding *pinyin* and English words.

1 清扫	sǎ	water
2 浸泡	qīngsǎo	sweep
3 洒	shuǐ	soak
4 水	jìnpào	spray

2. 词语搭配连线。Match the words.

1 洒	地板
	水
2 清扫	料槽
	围栏

学习课文 Text 8-2

Qīngsǎo juànshè
清扫圈舍

Xiān yòng sàozhou qīngsǎo dìbǎn, liàocáo hé wéilán, ránhòu yòng

先用扫帚清扫地板、料槽和围栏，然后用

tiěchǎn qīnglǐ wūwù.
铁铲清理污物。

Nán qīnglǐ de wūwù, kěyǐ xiān sǎ shuǐ, jìnpào, ránhòu yòng
难清理的污物，可以先洒水、浸泡，然后用
tiěchǎn qīnglǐ.
铁铲清理。

Sweeping Animal Pens

First, use a broom to clean the floor, feeding troughs and fences. Then use a shovel to clean dirt. For the dirt that is hard to clean , you can first spray water to soak it and then use a shovel to clean it away.

课文练习 Text Exercises

1. 选词填空。Fill in the blanks with the correct words.

A 洒水	B 清扫	C 清理

1. 先用扫帚________地板、料槽和围栏。
2. 然后用铁铲________污物。
3. 难清理的污物，可以先________、浸泡，然后用铁铲清理。

2. 判断正误。True or false.

1. 我们用铁铲清扫地板、料槽和围栏。
2. 我们用扫帚清扫地板、料槽和围栏。
3. 难清理的污物，可以先洒水、浸泡，然后用铁铲清理。

学习语法 Grammar

语法点 1 Grammar Point 1

结构助词：的　Structural particle: 的

"的"一般用于定语后、名词前，是定语的标志。

It is an attributive marker usually used after an attribute and before a noun.

常用结构：名词 / 代词 / 形容词 / 动词 / 短语 + 的 + 名词

Common structure: noun / pronoun / adjective / verb / phrase + 的 + noun

例句：

1. Wǒ xiān qīnglǐ nán qīnglǐ de wūwù.
   我先清理难清理的污物。I will clean the dirt that is hard to clean.
2. Tā shì wǒmen gōngsī de yuángōng.
   他是我们公司的员工。He is the employee of our company.
3. Zhè shì wǒ de yǎnjìng.
   这是我的眼镜。These are my glasses.

语法练习 1 Grammar Exercise 1

替换练习。**Substitution drills.**

例句：我的工作服。

我 员工 他们	的	工作服 工作鞋 眼镜 耳机

语法点 2 Grammar Point 2

能愿动词：可以　Modal verb: 可以

能愿动词“可以”放在动词前面，表示某事可能或者能够发生，也可以表示主观上允许某事发生。否定形式是“不可以”，单独回答也可以说“不行”。

The modal verb “可以” is placed before a verb, indicating that something is possible to occur or capable of happening, or that something is subjectively allowed to occur. Its negative form is “不可以”, and when responding individually, one can simply say “不行”.

常用结构：主语 + 可以 + 动词性短语

Common structure: subject + 可以 + verb phrase

例句：

1. Nán qīnglǐ de wūwù, kěyǐ xiān sǎ shuǐ, jìnpào, zài yòng tiěchǎn qīnglǐ.
   难清理的污物，可以先洒水、浸泡，再用铁铲清理。
   For the dirt which is difficult to clean, you can first spray water to soak it, and then use a shovel to clean it up.
2. Nǐ kěyǐ zài gēngyīshì tuōxia gōngzuòfú.
   你可以在更衣室脱下工作服。You can take off your working clothes in the locker room.
3. Wǒ kěyǐ jìnlai ma?
   我可以进来 (come in) 吗？ May I come in?

语法练习 2 Grammar Exercise 2

根据课文内容给下列说法排序。Put the statements in the correct order according to the text.

1. ①他们　②进入养殖场　③可以

   ____

2. ①在更衣室更衣　②员工　③可以

   ____

3 ①我们 ②可以 ③用紫外线灯消毒

4 ①用酒精擦拭随身物品 ②可以 ③我们

汉字书写 Writing Chinese Characters

rén 人

dà 大

tài 太

quǎn 犬

文化拓展 Culture Insight

Confucius

Confucius was a Chinese philosopher and politician of the Spring and

Autumn period, and he is China's most famous educator. The philosophy of Confucius, also known as Confucianism, emphasizes personal and governmental morality, the correctness of social relationships, justice, kindness, and sincerity. *The Analects of Confucius* is regarded as a Confucian classic, which records the words and deeds of Confucius and his disciples.

小结 Summary

词语 Words

朗读词语。Read the words aloud.

清扫	扫帚	地板	料槽	围栏
铁铲	污物	难	的	可以
洒	水	浸泡		

语法 Grammar

语言点回顾。Language points review.

语言点	常用结构	例句
结构助词：的	N / Pron / Adj / V / Phrase + 的 + N	我先清理难清理的污物。 他是我们公司的员工。

（续表）

语言点	常用结构	例句
能愿动词：可以	S + 可以 + VP	难清理的污物，可以先洒水、浸泡，再用铁铲清理。 我可以进来吗？

课文理解 Text Comprehension

根据提示复述课文。Retell the text according to the prompts.

先用扫帚清扫________、________和________，然后用________清理污物。难清理的污物，可以先________、浸泡，然后用铁铲________。

第9课 Lesson 9

Zuòhǎo fánghù
做好防护
Taking Protective Measures

复习 Revision

朗读句子。Read the sentences aloud.

1 用消毒液擦拭随身物品。

2 用紫外线灯消毒。

3 用扫帚清扫地板、料槽和围栏。

4 用铁铲清理污物。

热身 Warming Up

看图选词。Look at the pictures and choose the correct words.

A kǒuzhào 口罩 mask	B hùmùjìng 护目镜 goggles
C ěrsāi 耳塞 earplugs	D xiàngjiāo shǒutào 橡胶手套 rubber gloves

1

2
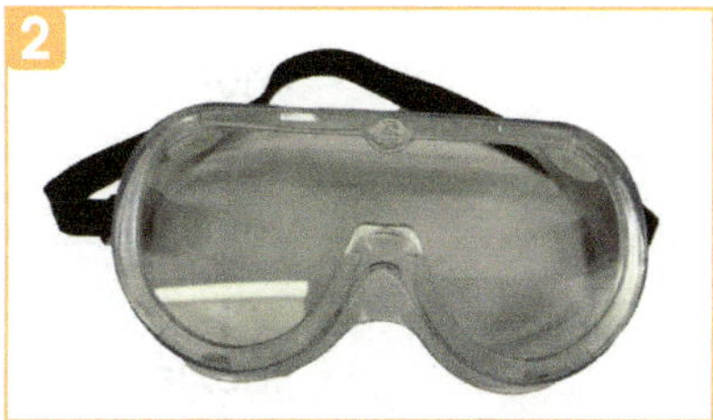

3
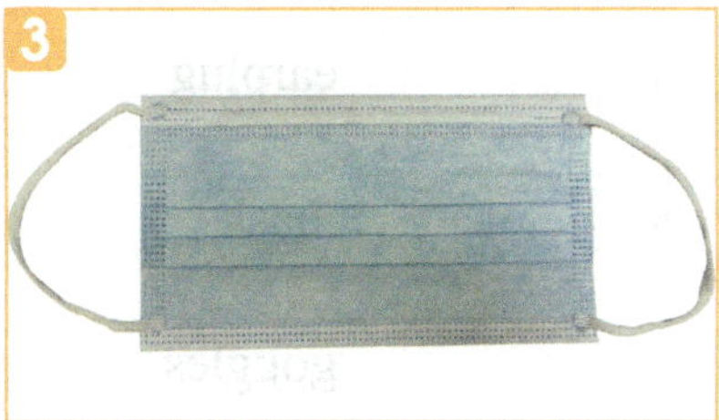

4
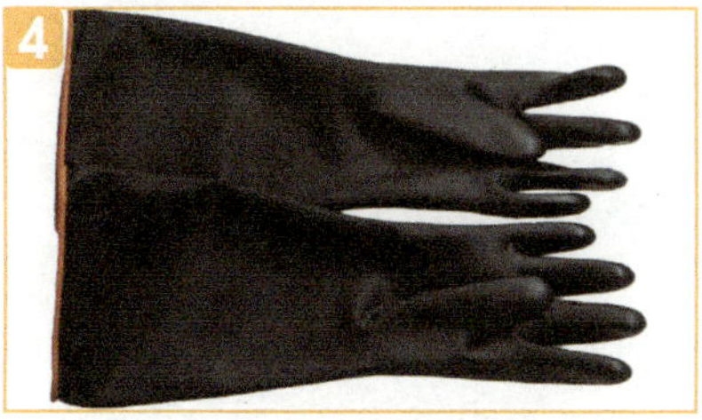

学习生词 Words and Expressions 9-1

1	做	zuò	*v.*	do
2	好	hǎo	*adj.*	good to (do)
3	防护	fánghù	*v.*	protect
4	喷洒	pēnsǎ	*v.*	spray
5	泡沫	pàomò	*n.*	foam
6	清洁剂	qīngjiéjì		cleaner
7	前	qián	*n.*	past; former times
8	注意	zhùyì	*v.*	pay attention to
9	安全	ānquán	*adj.*	safe

10	雨衣	yǔyī	*n.*	raincoat
11	雨裤	yǔkù		rain pants
12	胶鞋	jiāoxié	*n.*	rubber shoes
13	戴	dài	*v.*	wear
14	耳塞	ěrsāi	*n.*	earplug
15	口罩	kǒuzhào	*n.*	mask
16	护目镜	hùmùjìng		goggles
17	橡胶	xiàngjiāo	*n.*	rubber
18	手套	shǒutào	*n.*	glove

词语练习 Words Exercises

1. 将中文词语和对应的拼音及英文连线。Match the Chinese words with corresponding *pinyin* and English.

1 喷洒	fánghù	pay attention to
2 防护	ānquán	safe
3 注意	zhùyì	spray
4 安全	pēnsǎ	protect

2. 选词填空。Fill in the blanks with the correct words.

A 穿　　　　B 戴

1 ________雨衣　　2 ________口罩

3 ________雨裤　　4 ________耳塞

5 ________胶鞋　　6 ________护目镜

学习课文 Text 9-2

Zuòhǎo fánghù
做好防护

Pēnsǎ pàomò qīngjiéjì qián, yào zuòhǎo fánghù, zhùyì ānquán.
喷洒泡沫清洁剂前，要做好防护，注意安全。

Yào chuānhǎo yǔyī, yǔkù, jiāoxié, dàihǎo ěrsāi, kǒuzhào, hùmùjìng, zuìhòu dàihǎo xiàngjiāo shǒutào.
要穿好雨衣、雨裤、胶鞋，戴好耳塞、口罩、护目镜，最后戴好橡胶手套。

Taking Protective Measures

Before spraying foam cleaner, take protective measures and pay attention to safety. Put on a raincoat, rain pants, and rubber shoes. Wear earplugs, a mask, and goggles. Finally, put on rubber gloves.

课文练习 Text Exercises

1. 选词填空。Fill in the blanks with the correct words.

A 戴好　　B 穿好　　C 做好　　D 注意

1 ________雨衣、雨裤、胶鞋。

2 ________耳塞、口罩、护目镜。

3 ________防护。

4 ________安全。

2. 判断正误。True or false.

1 喷洒泡沫清洁剂前，要戴好耳塞、口罩、护目镜。

2 喷洒泡沫清洁剂前，要穿好雨衣、雨裤、胶鞋。

3 喷洒泡沫清洁剂前，先要戴好橡胶手套。

4 喷洒泡沫清洁剂前，要做好防护，注意安全。

学习语法 Grammar

语法点 1 Grammar Point 1

固定格式：……前　Fixed structure: ……前

表示早于某个特定的时间发生了某事。

It indicates something happens before a specific time.

常用结构：动词性短语 + 前

Common structure: verb phrase + 前

例句：1 Pēnsǎ pàomò xiāodújì qián, yào chuānhǎo yǔyī.
喷洒泡沫消毒剂前，要穿好雨衣。Put on a raincoat before spraying foam cleaner.

2 Pēnsǎ pàomò qīngjiéjì qián, yào dàihǎo ěrsāi, kǒuzhào, hùmùjìng.
喷洒泡沫清洁剂前，要戴好耳塞、口罩、护目镜。
Wear earplugs, a mask and goggles before spraying foam cleaner.

3 Bǎowēndēng fàngrù wùliàojiān qián, qǐng yòng xiāodúyè cāshì xiāodú.
保温灯放入物料间前，请用消毒液擦拭消毒。Please disinfect the heat lamps with disinfectant before putting them into the material room.

语法练习 1 Grammar Exercise 1

用"……前"改写句子。Rewrite the sentences with "……前".

1 进入养殖场　　要洗澡和消毒

________前，________。

2 我们脱下工作服　　出养殖场

________前，________。

3 先用扫帚清扫地板　　用铁铲清理污物

________前，________。

4 用消毒液擦拭消毒　　保温灯放入物料间

________前，________。

语法点 2 Grammar Point 2

结果补语：动词＋好　Complement of result: verb + 好

补语是补充说明谓语的成分，放在谓语动词的后面。用来描述动作或行为的结果或状态的补语是结果补语。

A complement is a component that supplements and explains the predicate, placed after the predicate verb. A complement that is used to describe the result or state of an action or behavior is called a complement of result.

常用结构：动词 + 好

Common structure: verb + 好

例句：1 Chuānhǎo yǔyī, dàihǎo ěrsāi, zuòhǎo fánghù.
穿好雨衣、戴好耳塞、做好防护。Put on a raincoat, wear the earplugs, and ensure adequate protection.

2 Xiāodú hǎo suíshēn wùpǐn.
消毒好随身物品。Disinfect all personal belongings thoroughly.

3 Zhěnglǐ hǎo juànshè.
整理好圈舍。Tidy up the animal pens.

语法练习 2 Grammar Exercise 2

替换练习。Substitution drills.

例句：穿好工作服。

穿 戴	好	工作服 雨衣 胶鞋 口罩 耳塞 橡胶手套

汉字书写 Writing Chinese Characters

shàng 上上上

上 上 上 上 上

xià 下下下

下 下 下 下 下

zuǒ 左左左左左

左 左 左 左 左

yòu 右右右右右

右 右 右 右 右

职业拓展 Career Insight

The Production Safety of Livestock and Poultry Farms

The production safety of livestock and poultry farms involves multiple aspects, mainly including facility safety, water and electricity safety, sanitation and disinfection, feed and drug management, animal epidemic prevention, manure and sewage treatment, personnel safety, as well as emergency preparedness and response. Overall, the production safety of livestock and poultry farms requires comprehensive management and control from multiple perspectives, including infrastructure, animal epidemic prevention, manure and sewage treatment, feed and drug management, as well as personnel safety. By strengthening safety management in these areas, it can ensure that the production activities of livestock and poultry farms are carried out safely and efficiently, providing strong guarantees for the healthy growth of livestock and poultry and the quality and safety of products.

小结 Summary

词语 Words

选择正确的答案。Choose the correct answers.

A 雨衣	B 橡胶手套	C 雨裤	D 口罩
E 胶鞋	F 护目镜	G 耳塞	

1 穿 A ______

2 戴 B ______

语法 Grammar

语言点回顾。Language points review.

语言点	常用结构	例句
固定格式： ……前	VP + 前	喷洒泡沫消毒剂前，要穿好雨衣。 喷洒泡沫清洁剂前，要戴好耳塞、口罩、护目镜。

（续表）

语言点	常用结构	例句
结果补语： 动词＋好	V＋好	穿好雨衣、戴好耳塞、做好防护。 消毒好随身物品。

课文理解 Text Comprehension

根据提示复述课文。Retell the text according to the prompts.

喷洒泡沫清洁剂前，要做好________，注意________。要穿好________、________、________，戴好________、________、________，最后戴好________。

第10课 Lesson 10

Zǔzhuāng qīngxǐ gōngjù
组装清洗工具
Assembling the Cleaning Tools

复习 Revision

根据提示练习说句子。**Practice speaking sentences according to the prompts.**

喷洒泡沫清洁剂前，要穿好________、________、________，戴好________、________、________，最后戴好________。

热身 Warming Up

看图选词。**Look at the pictures and choose the correct words.**

A 水桶 (shuǐtǒng) bucket

B 高压清洗机 (gāoyā qīngxǐjī) high-pressure cleaning machine

C 高压水枪 (gāoyā shuǐqiāng) high-pressure water gun

D 高压水管 (gāoyā shuǐguǎn) high-pressure water pipe

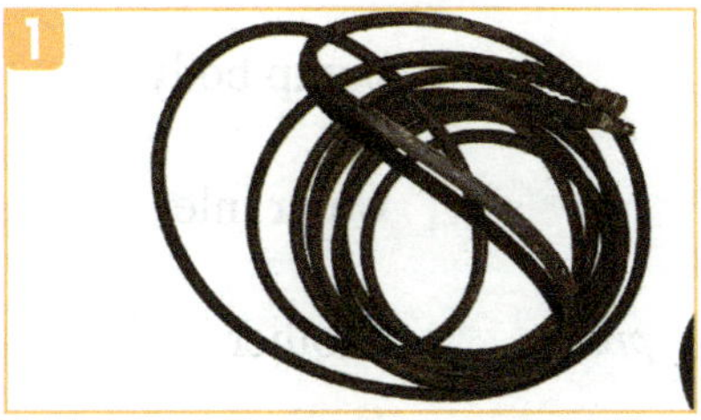

学习生词 Words and Expressions 10-1

1	组装	zǔzhuāng	*v.*	assemble
2	清洗	qīngxǐ	*v.*	rinse
3	工具	gōngjù	*n.*	tool
4	准备	zhǔnbèi	*v.*	prepare
5	大	dà	*adj.*	big; large
6	水桶	shuǐtǒng		bucket
7	装满	zhuāngmǎn		fill up
8	连接	liánjiē	*v.*	connect
9	进水管	jìnshuǐguǎn		water inlet pipe

10	泵体	bèngtǐ		pump body
11	进水口	jìnshuǐkǒu		water inlet
12	另外	lìngwài	*pron.*	another
13	端	duān		end
14	放	fàng	*v.*	place; put
15	里	lǐ	*n.*	inside
16	高压水管	gāoyā shuǐguǎn		high-pressure water pipe
17	高压水枪	gāoyā shuǐqiāng		high-pressure water gun
18	拧	nǐng	*v.*	screw; twist
19	紧	jǐn	*adj.*	tight
20	高压清洗机	gāoyā qīngxǐjī		high-pressure cleaning machine
21	各	gè	*pron.*	every; all; each
22	接口	jiēkǒu	*n.*	connector

词语练习 Words Exercises

1. 将中文词语和对应的拼音及英文连线。**Match the Chinese words with corresponding *pinyin* and English words.**

1	拧紧	liánjiē	place; put
2	准备	zhǔnbèi	connect
3	放	nǐngjǐn	prepare
4	连接	fàng	tighten

2. 词语分类。**Categorize the words.**

A 高压清洗机	B 保温灯	C 水桶	D 补料槽
E 高压水管	F 插座	G 高压水枪	

清洗工具的词语（words for cleaning tools）：

____

学习课文 Text 10-2

Zǔzhuāng qīngxǐ gōngjù
组装清洗工具

Zhǔnbèi yí ge dà shuǐtǒng, zhuāngmǎn shuǐ. Liánjiē jìnshuǐguǎn hé bèngtǐ jìnshuǐkǒu, jìnshuǐguǎn lìngwài yìduān fàng zài shuǐtǒng li. Gāoyā shuǐguǎn yìduān liánjiē bèngtǐ, lìngwài yìduān liánjiē gāoyā shuǐqiāng. Zuìhòu nǐngjǐn gāoyā qīngxǐjī gègè jiēkǒu.

准备一个大水桶，装满水。连接进水管和泵体进水口，进水管另外一端放在水桶里。高压水管一端连接泵体，另外一端连接高压水枪。最后拧紧高压清洗机各个接口。

Assembling the Cleaning Tools

Prepare a large bucket and fill it up with water. Connect the water inlet pipe to the water inlet of the pump body, and put the other end of the pipe in the bucket. Connect one end of the high-pressure water pipe to the pump body and connect the other end to the high-pressure water gun. At last, Tighten all connectors of the high-pressure cleaning machine.

课文练习 Text Exercises

1. 选词填空。Fill in the blanks with the correct words.

A 放　　B 连接　　C 拧紧　　D 准备

1. ________高压清洗机各个接口。
2. ________一个大水桶，装满水。
3. 进水管另外一端________在水桶里。
4. 高压水管一端________在泵体上。

2. 根据课文内容给下列说法排序。Put the statements in the correct order according to the text.

1. 连接进水管跟泵体进水口，进水管另外一端放在水桶里。
2. 拧紧高压清洗机各个接口。
3. 高压水管一端连接在泵体上，另外一端连接在高压水枪上。
4. 准备一个大水桶，装满水。

____

学习语法 Grammar

语法点 1 Grammar Point 1

指示代词：各　Demonstrative pronoun: 各

“各”指某一范围内所有的个体，常与量词连用，也可直接修饰名词，多与组织、机构等名词直接连用。

The word “各” refers to all individuals within a certain scope. It is often used together with a measure word, or can directly modify a noun. It is frequently used in direct conjunction with nouns referring to organizations, institutions, and the like.

常用结构：各 + 量词 / 名词

Common structure: 各 + measure word / noun

例句：

1. Nǐngjǐn gāoyā qīngxǐjī gègè jiēkǒu.
拧紧高压清洗机各个接口。
2. Xièxie gèwèi lǎoshī.
谢谢各位老师。Thank you, teachers.
3. Gèwèi, dàjiā hǎo!
各位，大家好！ Hello, everyone.

语法练习 1 Grammar Exercise 1

词语搭配连线。Match the words.

1 各 •	• 套（set） •	• 家禽
2 各 •	• 位 •	• 接口
3 各 •	• 种（species） •	• 员工
4 各 •	• 个 •	• 设备

语法点 2 Grammar Point 2

结果补语：动词 + 形容词　Complement of result: verb + adjective

结果补语主要用于描述动作或行为导致的结果，其中补语与述语之间是补充与被补充、说明与被说明的关系。

The Complement of result is mainly used to describe the result of an action or behavior, where the relationship between the complement and the statement is the relationship between the complement and the supplemented, and the explanation and the illustrated.

常用结构：动词 + 形容词（好、满、紧）

Common structure: verb + adjective (好 / 满 / 紧)

例句：

1. Qǐng chuānhǎo yǔyī, dàihǎo ěrsāi, zuòhǎo fánghù.
请 穿好雨衣、戴好耳塞、做好防护。Please put on the raincoat, wear the earplugs, and take protective measures.

2. Zhǔnbèi yí ge dà shuǐtǒng, zhuāngmǎn shuǐ.
准备一个大水桶，装满 水。Prepare a large bucket and fill it up with water.

3. Nǐngjǐn gāoyā qīngxǐjī gègè jiēkǒu.
拧紧高压清洗机各个接口。Tighten all connectors of the high-pressure cleaning machine.

语法练习 2 Grammar Exercise 2

选词填空。**Fill in the blanks with the correct words.**

A 好　　　B 紧　　　C 满

1. 穿________雨衣、戴好耳塞、做好防护。
2. 准备一个大水桶，装________水。

3 拧________高压清洗机各个接口。

4 请做________防护。

汉字书写 Writing Chinese Characters

rì 日 日 日 日

日 日 日 日 日

yuè 月 月 月 月

月 月 月 月 月

míng 明 明 明 明 明 明 明 明

明 明 明 明 明

péng 朋 朋 朋 朋 朋 朋 朋 朋

朋 朋 朋 朋 朋

文化拓展 Culture Insight

The Water-Sprinkling Festival of the Dai Nationality

The Water-Sprinkling Festival, a traditional festival celebrated by the Dai nationality in Yunnan Province, China, falls in the middle of June according to the Dai calendar. People dress in their holiday costumes, stroll through the streets, splash water on each other as a way to convey blessings. Additionally, they engage in activities such as bathing the Buddha, dragon boat racing, and performing the peacock dance.

小结 Summary

词语 Words

朗读词语。**Read the words aloud.**

组装	清洗	工具
准备	水桶	连接
另外	拧紧	接口

语法 Grammar

语言点回顾。**Language points review.**

语言点	常用结构	例句
指示代词：各	各 + M / N	拧紧高压清洗机各个接口。 谢谢各位。
结果补语：动词 + 形容词	V + Adj	准备一个大水桶，装满水。 请做好防护。

课文理解 Text Comprehension

根据提示复述课文。Retell the text according to the prompts.

准备一个大________，装满水。连接进水管和泵体________，进水管________一端放在水桶里。高压水管________连接泵体，另外一端连接________。最后________高压清洗机各个________。

第11课 Lesson 11

Zǔzhuāng pēnsǎ shèbèi
组装喷洒设备
Assembling the Spraying Equipment

复习 Revision

朗读句子。**Read the sentences aloud.**

1 各位朋友，大家好！

2 请穿好雨衣、戴好耳塞、做好防护。

3 准备一个大水桶，装满水。

4 拧紧高压清洗机各个接口。

热身 Warming Up

看图选词。**Look at the pictures and choose the correct words.**

A 比例 (bǐlì) proportion	B 喷壶 (pēnhú) spray bottle
C 旋转 (xuánzhuǎn) rotate	D 泡沫 (pàomò) foam

1

2

3

4

学习生词 Words and Expressions 11-1

1	方法	fāngfǎ	*n.*	method
2	喷壶	pēnhú	*n.*	spray bottle
3	再	zài	*adv.*	then
4	按照	ànzhào	*prep.*	according to
5	比例	bǐlì	*n.*	ratio; proportion
6	要求	yāoqiú	*n.*	requirement
7	旋转	xuánzhuǎn	*v.*	rotate
8	旋钮	xuánniǔ		knob
9	调节	tiáojié	*v.*	adjust

词语练习 Words Exercises

1. 将中文词语和对应的拼音及英文连线。Match the Chinese words with corresponding *pinyin* and English words.

1 按照	pēnsǎ	rotate
2 喷洒	ànzhào	according to
3 旋转	tiáojié	adjust
4 调节	xuánzhuǎn	spray

2. 词语搭配连线。Match the words.

1 组装	要求
2 按照	清洁剂
3 旋转	旋钮
4 装满	设备

学习课文 Text 11-2

Zǔzhuāng pēnsǎ shèbèi
组装 喷洒设备

Zǔzhuāng pēnsǎ shèbèi de fāngfǎ:
组装 喷洒设备的方法：

Xiān zài pēnhú li zhuāngmǎn pàomò qīngjiéjì, zài liánjiē pēnhú hé gāoyā shuǐqiāng, zuìhòu ànzhào pàomò qīngjiéjì hé shuǐ de bǐlì yāoqiú xuánzhuǎn pēnhú xuánniǔ, tiáojié pàomò qīngjiéjì hé shuǐ de pēnsǎ bǐlì.
先在喷壶里 装满 泡沫清洁剂，再连接喷壶和高压水枪，最后按照泡沫清洁剂和水的比例要求 旋转喷壶旋钮，调节泡沫清洁剂和水的喷洒比例。

Assembling the Spraying Equipment

The method of assembling spraying equipment:

First, fill up the spray bottle with foam cleaner, and then connect the spray bottle to the high-pressure water gun, finally, rotate the spray bottle knob according to the required ratio of foam cleaner to water to adjust the ratio of the mixture.

课文练习 Text Exercises

1. 选词填空。Fill in the blanks with the correct words.

A 调节	B 装满	C 按照	D 连接

1. 在喷壶里________泡沫清洁剂。
2. ________喷壶和高压水枪。
3. ________要求旋转喷壶旋钮。
4. ________泡沫清洁剂和水的喷洒比例。

2. 根据课文内容给下列说法排序。Put the statements in the correct order according to the text.

1. 按照要求旋转喷壶旋钮。
2. 在喷壶里装满泡沫清洁剂。
3. 调节泡沫清洁剂和水的喷洒比例。
4. 连接喷壶和高压水枪。

____

学习语法 Grammar

语法点 1 Grammar Point 1

关联副词：再　Correlative adverb: 再

关联副词“再”表示两个动作的先后承接。常与“先”组成“先……，再……”结构。“再”常用连接两个动词性短语，第一个动词性短语前可以加“先”，前后两个动作的主语可以相同，也可以不同。

The correlative adverb “再” indicates the sequence of two actions. It is often used with “先” to form the structure “先……, 再……”.The word “再” is often used to connect two verb phrases. “先” can be added before the first verb phrase. The subjects of the two actions can be the same or different.

常用结构：主语 1（+ 先）+ 动词性短语 1（+ 主语 2 / 主语 1）+ 再 + 动词性短语 2

Common structure: subject 1 (+ 先) + verb phrase 1 (+ subject 2 / subject 1) + 再 + verb phrase 2

例句：

1. Wǒ xiān liánjiē pēnhú hé gāoyā shuǐqiāng, zài liánjiē gāoyā shuǐqiāng hé shuǐguǎn.
我先连接喷壶和高压水枪，再连接高压水枪和水管。
First, I connected the spray bottle to the high-pressure water gun, and then connected the high-pressure water gun to the water pipe.

2. Xiān yízǒu shèbèi, zài guānbì diànyuán.
先移走设备，再关闭电源。Remove the equipment first, and then turn off the power.

3. Wǒ xiān qīngsǎo dìbǎn, zài qīngsǎo liàocáo.
我先清扫地板，再清扫料槽。I will clean the floor first, and then clean the trough.

语法练习 1 Grammar Exercise 1

替换练习。Substitution drills.

例句：我先移走设备，再关闭电源。

我	移走设备	关闭电源。
	穿工作服	消毒随身物品。
	清扫地板	清扫料槽。
	洒水、浸泡污物	用铁铲清理。

语法点 2 Grammar Point 2

介词：按照　Preposition: 按照

介词“按照”后面通常跟名词组成介词结构，表示遵从某种标准。

The preposition “ 按照 ” is usually followed by a noun to form a prepositional phrase. It means following a certain standard.

常用结构：主语 + 按照 + 名词性短语 + 动词性短语

Common structure: subject + 按照 + noun phrase + verb phrase

例句：

1. Wǒmen yào ànzhào pàomò qīngjiéjì hé shuǐ de bǐlì yāoqiú xuánzhuǎn pēnhú xuánniǔ.
我们要按照泡沫清洁剂和水的比例要求旋转喷壶旋钮。
We should rotate the spray bottle knob according to the required ratio of foam cleaner to water.

2. Dàwèi ànzhào yāoqiú xiāodú suíshēn wùpǐn.
大卫按照要求消毒随身物品。David disinfected the belongings as required.

3. Lǐ Shān ànzhào wǒ de fāngfǎ, zǔzhuāng pēnsǎ shèbèi.
李山按照我的方法，组装喷洒设备。Li Shan assembled the spraying equipment according to my method.

语法练习 2 Grammar Exercise 2

按照正确的语序连词成句。Make sentences in correct orders with the given words or phrases.

1 ①按照泡沫清洁剂和水的比例要求 ②旋转喷壶旋钮 ③我

____

2 ①大卫 ②按照要求 ③调节泡沫清洁剂和水的比例

____

3 ①组装喷洒设备 ②按照我的方法 ③他

____

4 ①大卫 ②消毒随身物品 ③按照要求

____

汉字书写 Writing Chinese Characters

mù

木	木	木	木	木						

běn

本	本	本	本	本						

shù

术	术	术	术	术						

hé 禾禾禾禾禾

禾	禾	禾	禾	禾						

文化拓展 Culture Insight

Laozi

Laozi was an ancient Chinese philosopher and writer, reputed to be the author of the *Tao Te Ching* and considered the founder of Taoism. Taoism differs from Confucianism in its non-emphasis on rigid rituals and social order. Taoism emphasizes naturalness. The essence of Taoism thought can be summarized as "governing by non-action" and "following the way of nature".

小结 Summary

词语 Words

替换练习。**Substitution drills.**

例句：连接喷壶和高压水枪

连接	喷壶 高压水枪 水管

语法 Grammar

语言点回顾。Language points review.

语言点	常用结构	例句
关联副词：再	S_1（+ 先）+ VP_1（+ S_2 / S_1）+ 再 + VP_2	我先连接喷壶和高压水枪，再连接高压水枪和水管。 请先移走设备，再关闭电源。
介词：按照	S + 按照 + NP + VP	我们要按照泡沫清洁剂和水的比例要求旋转喷壶旋钮。 大卫按照要求消毒随身物品。

课文理解 Text Comprehension

根据提示复述课文。Retell the text according to the prompts.

组装喷洒设备的方法：先在喷壶里________泡沫清洁剂，再________喷壶和高压水枪，最后________泡沫清洁剂和水的________要求旋转喷壶________，________泡沫清洁剂和水的________比例。

第12课 Lesson 12

Pēnsǎ pàomò qīngjiéjì
喷洒泡沫清洁剂
Spraying the Foam Cleaner

复习 Revision

朗读句子。Read the sentences aloud.

1 我先连接喷壶和高压水枪，再连接高压水枪和水管。

2 请先移走设备，再关闭电源。

3 我们要按照泡沫清洁剂和水的比例要求旋转喷壶旋钮。

4 大卫按照要求消毒随身物品。

热身 Warming Up

看图选词。Look at the pictures and choose the correct words.

A chōngxǐ 冲洗 rinse	B shǒu 手 hand
C bānjī 扳机 trigger	D chǎnchuáng 产床 maternity pen

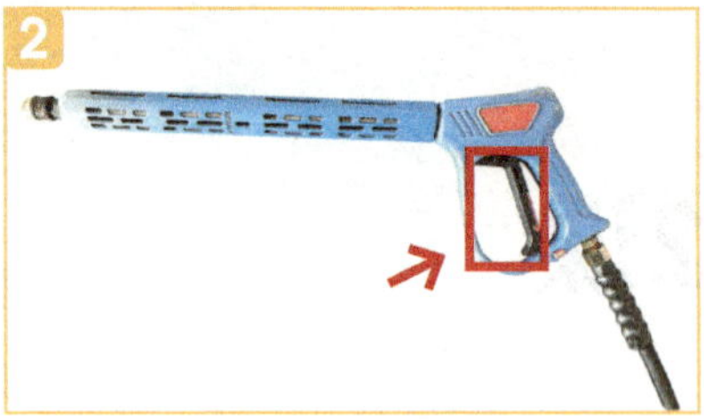

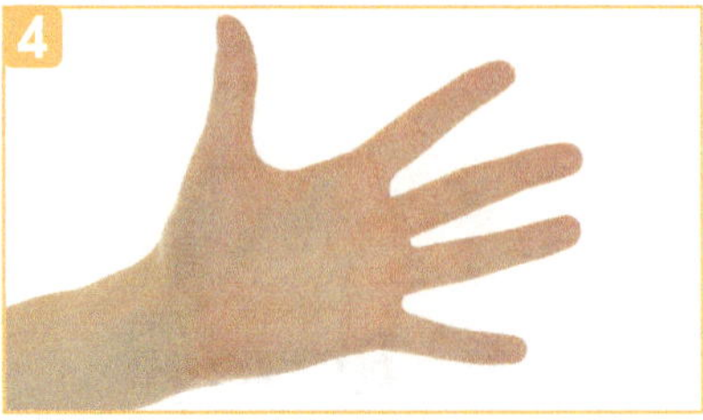

学习生词 Words and Expressions 12-1

1	步骤	bùzhòu	*n.*	step
2	双	shuāng	*adj.*	two; twain; double
3	手	shǒu	*n.*	hand
4	拿	ná	*v.*	take
5	对准	duìzhǔn		aim at
6	产床	chǎnchuáng	*n.*	maternity pen
7	位置	wèizhì	*n.*	position; location
8	其中	qízhōng	*n.*	among of them

9	只	zhī	*measure word*	measure word
10	按	àn	*v.*	press
11	扳机	bānjī	*n.*	trigger
12	均匀	jūnyún	*adj.*	even
13	分钟	fēnzhōng	*measure word*	minute
14	后	hòu	*n.*	later; after
15	冲洗	chōngxǐ	*v.*	rinse

词语练习 Words Exercises

1. 将中文词语和对应的拼音及英文连线。Match the Chinese words with corresponding *pinyin* and English words.

1 拿	àn	aim at
2 对准	ná	rinse
3 按	chōngxǐ	press
4 冲洗	duìzhǔn	take

2. 词语搭配连线。Match the words.

1 冲洗	位置
2 按	产床
3 对准	泡沫清洁剂
4 喷洒	扳机

学习课文 Text 12-2

Pēnsǎ pàomò qīngjiéjì
喷洒泡沫清洁剂

Pēnsǎ pàomò qīngjiéjì de bùzhòu:
喷洒泡沫清洁剂的步骤：

Shuāngshǒu ná gāoyā shuǐqiāng, duìzhǔn chǎnchuáng, wéilán, liàocáo děng wèizhi. Qízhōng yì zhī shǒu àn gāoyā shuǐqiāng bānjī, jūnyún pēnsǎ pàomò qīngjiéjì. Jìnpào shíwǔ dào sānshí fēnzhōng hòu, yòng gāoyā shuǐqiāng chōngxǐ.
双手拿高压水枪，对准产床、围栏、料槽等位置。其中一只手按高压水枪扳机，均匀喷洒泡沫清洁剂。浸泡15—30分钟后，用高压水枪冲洗。

Spraying the Foam Cleaner

Steps for spraying the foam cleaner:

Hold the high-pressure water gun with both hands, aiming at the position of the maternity pens, fences and feeding troughs. Press the trigger of the high-pressure water gun with one hand and spray the foam cleaner evenly. Soak for 15 to 30 minutes, and rinse with the high-pressure water gun.

课文练习 Text Exercises

1. 选词填空。Fill in the blanks with the correct words.

A 浸泡	B 对准	C 按	D 拿

1. 双手 ________ 高压水枪。
2. ________ 产床、围栏、料槽等位置。
3. 其中一只手 ________ 高压水枪扳机。
4. ________ 15—30 分钟后，用高压水枪冲洗。

2. 根据课文内容给下列说法排序。Put the statements in the correct order according to the text.

1. 浸泡 15—30 分钟后，用高压水枪冲洗。
2. 双手拿高压水枪。
3. 其中一只手按高压水枪扳机，均匀喷洒泡沫清洁剂。
4. 对准产床、围栏、料槽等位置。

____

学习语法 Grammar

语法点 1 Grammar Point 1

时量词 Temporal measure word

表示时间单位的量词称为时量词。时量词用在数词后面。汉语的时量词有“年、月、天、小时、分钟”等。时量词可以用在动词后面做时量补语，表示动作进行的时间。

The quantifier that represents a unit of time is called a temporal measure word. It is used after a numeral. In Chinese, temporal measure words include “年 (year)”, “月 (month)”, “天 (day)”, “小时 (hour)”, “分钟 (minute)”, etc. A temporal measure word can be used after a verb as a complement of time duration to indicate the length of time for which the action occurs.

常用结构：动词＋数词＋时量词

Common structure: verb + numeral + temporal measure word

例句：1 Jìnpào shíwǔ dào sānshí fēnzhōng.
浸泡 15—30 分钟。Soak for 15 to 30 minutes.

2 Xiāodú shíwǔ fēnzhōng.
消毒 15 分钟。Disinfect for 15 minutes.

3 Gōngzuò sānshí fēnzhōng.
工作 30 分钟。work for 30 minutes.

语法练习 1 Grammar Exercise 1

替换练习。Substitution drills.

例句：消毒 5 分钟。

消毒 工作 浸泡	5 分钟 15 分钟 30 分钟 45 分钟

语法点 2 Grammar Point 2

固定格式：……后　Fixed structure: ……后

“……后”表示晚于某个特定时间。时间词或动词性短语应放在“后”的前面。

It indicates a time later than a specific point in time. A time word or verb phrase should be placed before “……后”.

常用结构：动词 / 动词性短语 + 后，……

Common structure: verb / verb phrase + 后，……

例句：

1. Jìnpào shíwǔ dào sānshí fēnzhōnghòu, yòng gāoyā shuǐqiāng chōngxǐ.
浸泡 15—30 分钟后，用高压水枪冲洗。Soak for 15 to 30 minutes and then rinse with a high-pressure water gun.

2. Yòng xiāodúyè cāshì xiāodú hòu, fàngrù wùliàojiān.
用消毒液擦拭消毒后，放入物料间。Wipe and disinfect them with disinfectant, then put them into the material room.

3. Sǎ shuǐ, jìnpào hòu, yòng tiěchǎn qīnglǐ wūwù.
洒水、浸泡后，用铁铲清理污物。After spraying water and soaking, use a shovel to clear away the dirt.

语法练习 2 Grammar Exercise 2

按照正确的语序连词成句。Make sentences in correct orders with the given words or phrases.

1. ①浸泡 15—30 分钟后　②用高压水枪冲洗

____

2. ①进入洗澡间洗澡　②在内更衣室脱下工作服后

____

3. ①手机、耳机、眼镜等随身物品用消毒液擦拭、用紫外线灯消毒后　②出养殖场

____

4 ①连接喷壶和高压水枪 ②在喷壶里装满泡沫清洁剂后

____

汉字书写 Writing Chinese Characters

niú 牛 牛 牛 牛

牛	牛	牛	牛	牛						

shēng 生 生 生 生 生

生	生	生	生	生						

yáng 羊 羊 羊 羊 羊 羊

羊	羊	羊	羊	羊						

měi 美 美 美 美 美 美 美 美 美

美	美	美	美	美						

职业拓展 Career Insight

Drones for Pesticides Spraying

Using agricultural drones for pesticides spraying can enhance efficacy, reduce the usage of chemicals and water, save labor, effectively minimize soil pollution and pesticide residues, improve the effect of agricultural pest control, ensure the quality and safety of agricultural products, and enhance the application of science and technology in agriculture.

小结 Summary

词语 Words

朗读词语。Read the words aloud.

步骤	手	拿	对准	产床
位置	扳机	均匀	分钟	冲洗

语法 Grammar

语言点回顾。Language points review.

语言点	常用结构	例句
时量词	V + Num + M时	浸泡 15—30 分钟。 消毒 15 分钟。
固定格式：……后	V / VP + 后，……	浸泡 15—30 分钟后，用高压水枪冲洗。 用消毒液擦拭消毒后，放入物料间。

课文理解 Text Comprehension

根据提示复述课文。Retell the text according to the prompts.

喷洒泡沫清洁剂的步骤：________拿高压水枪，对准________、________、________等位置。其中一只手按高压水枪________，________喷洒泡沫清洁剂。浸泡________分钟后，用高压水枪________。

第13课 Lesson 13

Shǐyòng gāoyā shuǐqiāng
使用高压水枪
Using the High-Pressure Water Gun

复习 Revision

判断正误。**True or false.**

1 喷洒泡沫清洁剂前，要做好防护，注意安全。

2 喷洒泡沫清洁剂后，浸泡5—10分钟。

3 喷洒泡沫清洁剂后，不用高压水枪冲洗。

4 先用高压水枪冲洗，再喷洒泡沫清洁剂。

热身 Warming Up

看图选词。**Look at the pictures and choose the correct words.**

A 天花板 (tiānhuābǎn) ceiling	B 墙面 (qiángmiàn) wall
C 中间 (zhōngjiān) center; middle	D 水槽 (shuǐcáo) sink

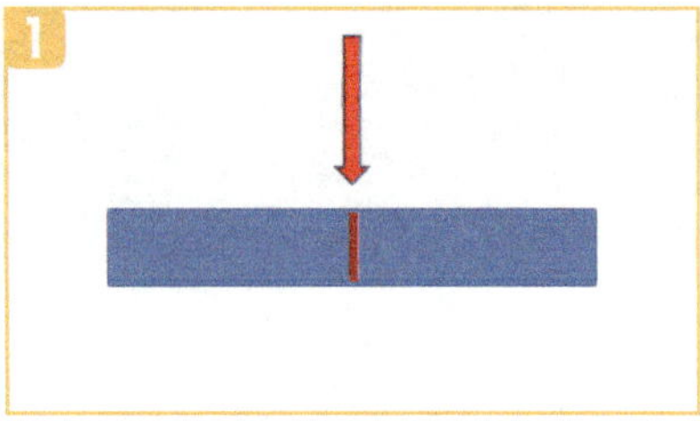

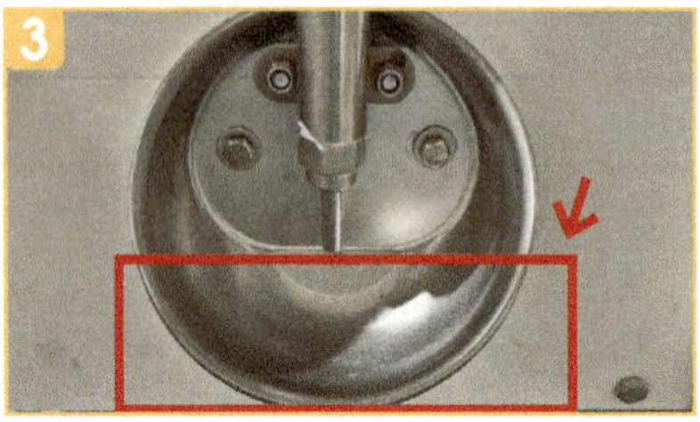

学习生词 Words and Expressions 13-1

1	使用	shǐyòng	*v.*	use
2	打开	dǎkāi		open; switch on
3	开关	kāiguān	*n.*	switch
4	握	wò	*v.*	hold
5	把手	bǎshou	*n.*	handle
6	中间	zhōngjiān	*n.*	center; middle
7	控制	kòngzhì	*v.*	control
8	方向	fāngxiàng	*n.*	direction
9	从……到……	cóng... dào...		from…to…

10	上	shàng	*n.*	high place; higher position
11	下	xià	*n.*	low position or rank
12	顺序	shùnxù	*n.*	order; sequence
13	天花板	tiānhuābǎn	*n.*	ceiling
14	墙面	qiángmiàn		wall
15	水槽	shuǐcáo		sink
16	设施	shèshī	*n.*	facility
17	冲力	chōnglì	*n.*	impact force

词语练习 Words Exercises

1. 将中文词语和对应的拼音及英文连线。Match the Chinese words with corresponding *pinyin* and English words.

1 顺序	fāngxiàng	direction
2 冲力	shùnxù	handle
3 把手	chōnglì	order; sequence
4 方向	bǎshou	impact force

2. 词语搭配连线。Match the words.

1 控制	把手
2 握好	顺序
3 按照	开关
4 打开	方向

学习课文 Text 13-2

Shǐyòng gāoyā shuǐqiāng
使用高压水枪

Zuòhǎo fánghù, dǎkāi gāoyā shuǐqiāng kāiguān, yì zhī shǒu wò gāoyā shuǐqiāng bǎshou, lìngwài yì zhī shǒu wò gāoyā shuǐqiāng de zhōngjiān wèizhi, kòngzhì chōngxǐ fāngxiàng.

做好防护，打开高压水枪开关，一只手握高压水枪把手，另外一只手握高压水枪的中间位置，控制冲洗方向。

Àn gāoyā shuǐqiāng bānjī, ànzhào cóng shàng dào xià, cóng lǐ dào wài de shùnxù chōngxǐ tiānhuābǎn, qiángmiàn, liàocáo, shuǐcáo, chǎnchuáng děng shèshī.

按高压水枪扳机，按照从上到下，从里到外的顺序冲洗天花板、墙面、料槽、水槽、产床等设施。

Gāoyā shuǐqiāng chōnglì hěn dà, yào zhùyì ānquán.

高压水枪冲力很大，要注意安全。

Using the High-Pressure Water Gun

Get well protected and switch on the high-pressure water gun. Hold the handle of the high-pressure water gun with one hand, and control the direction of rinsing by holding the middle of the high-pressure water gun with the other hand.

Press the high-pressure water gun trigger to rinse the ceiling, wall, feeding troughs, sinks, maternity pens, and other facilities from top to bottom, from inside to outside.

The high-pressure water gun has a high impact force, please pay attention to safety.

课文练习 Text Exercises

1. 选词填空。Fill in the blanks with the correct words.

A 按	B 握	C 打开	D 控制

1. ________高压水枪开关。
2. 一只手________高压水枪把手。
3. ________冲洗方向。
4. ________高压水枪扳机。

2. 根据课文内容给下列说法排序。Put the statements in the correct order according to the text.

1. 按高压水枪扳机。
2. 另一只手握高压水枪的中间位置。
3. 一只手握高压水枪把手。
4. 打开高压水枪开关。

____

学习语法 Grammar

语法点 1 Grammar Point 1

方位名词 Nouns of locality

常用结构：（名词 + ）上 / 下 / 前 / 后 / 里 / 外

Common structure: (noun +) 上 / 下 / 前 / 后 / 里 / 外

表格中的词是一些常见的方位词。

Some common nouns of locality are in the table.

上	下	前	后	里	外
above	under	front	behind	inside	outside

例句：

1. Xiàngjiāo shǒutào zài wéilán shang.
橡胶 手套在围栏 上。Rubber gloves are on the fence.

2. Bàngōnglóu qián shì xiǎo guǎngchǎng.
办公楼前是小 广场。In front of the office building is a small square.

3. Sùshè lǐ méiyǒu rén.
宿舍里没有人。There is no one in the dormitory.

语法练习 1 Grammar Exercise 1

按照正确的语序连词成句。**Make sentences in correct orders with the given words or phrases.**

1. ①我 ②宿舍 ③在 ④里

____

2. ①橡胶手套 ②在 ③上 ④围栏

____

3 ①办公楼 ②前 ③小广场 ④是

____

4 ①小广场 ②是 ③后 ④办公楼

____

语法点 2 Grammar Point 2

固定格式：从……到……　Fixed structure: 从……到……

"从……到……"连接时间词或者处所词，表示时间或者处所的起点和终点。

Fixed structure "从……到…… (From…to…)" connects words of time or place, indicating the starting and ending points of time or place.

常用结构：从＋时间 / 处所＋到＋时间 / 处所

Common structure: 从＋time / location＋到＋time / location

例句：

1. Ànzhào cóng shàng dào xià, cóng lǐ dào wài de shùnxù chōngxǐ tiānhuābǎn.
按照从上到下、从里到外的顺序冲洗天花板。Wash the ceiling from top to bottom and from inside to outside.
2. Ànzhào cóng tiānhuābǎn dào dìmiàn de shùnxù xiāodú juànshè.
按照从天花板到地面的顺序消毒圈舍。Disinfect the animal pens in the order from the ceiling to the ground.
3. Cóng qián dào hòu qīnglǐ gānjìng.
从前到后清理干净。Clean up from front to back.

语法练习 2 Grammar Exercise 2

根据提示完成句子。**Complete the sentences according to the prompts.**

上 → 下

1 从__________________到__________________。

里 → 外

2 从________到________。

天花板 → 地面

3 从________到________。

北京 → 上海

4 从________到________。

汉字书写 Writing Chinese Characters

rì 日 日 日 日

日	日	日	日	日						

dàn 旦 旦 旦 旦 旦

旦	旦	旦	旦	旦						

zǎo 早 早 早 早 早 早

早	早	早	早	早						

xīng 星 星 星 星 星 星 星 星 星

星	星	星	星	星						

职业拓展 Career Insight

The High-Pressure Water Gun

The high-pressure water gun, also known as a high-pressure cleaning machine or high-pressure water jet cleaner, is a machine that utilizes a power unit to drive a high-pressure plunger pump, generating high-pressure water to rinse the surface of objects. It can effectively remove and wash away dirt, achieving the purpose of cleaning the surfaces. The power of the high-pressure water gun primarily originates from a diesel engine or an electric motor, which either bridges to or directly drives the operation.

小结 Summary

词语 Words

朗读词语。Read the words aloud.

使用	开关	把手	中间	控制
方向	顺序	天花板	墙面	水槽

语法 Grammar

语言点回顾。Language points review.

语言点	常用结构	例句
方位名词	（N＋）上／下／前／后／里／外	橡胶手套在围栏上。 办公楼前是操场。
固定格式：从……到……	从＋时间／处所＋到＋时间／处所	按照从上到下、从里到外的顺序冲洗天花板。 按照从天花板到地面的顺序消毒圈舍。

课文理解 Text Comprehension

根据提示复述课文。Retell the text according to the prompts.

做好________，打开高压水枪________。一只手握高压水枪________，另一只手握高压水枪的________位置，控制冲洗________。按高压水枪________，按照从________到________，从________到________的顺序冲洗天花板、墙面、料槽、水槽、产床等________。高压水枪________很大，要注意________。

第14课

Lesson 14

Jìsuàn yòngliàng
计算用量
Calculating the Amount

复习 Revision

根据提示使用固定格式“从……到……”。Use the fixed structure “从……到……” according to the prompts.

1 上　下

____

2 前　后

____

3 里　外

____

4 公司　养殖场

____

热身 Warming Up

认读词语。Learn and read the words.

1 róngyè 溶液 solution

2 yàopǐn 药品 medicine

3 xūyào 需要 need

4 lìrú 例如 take for example

5 háoshēng 毫升 milliliter (mL)

6 kè 克 gram (g)

学习生词 Words and Expressions 14-1

1	计算	jìsuàn	*v.*	count; calculate
2	用量	yòngliàng		dosage; amount
3	配制	pèizhì	*v.*	prepare
4	总量	zǒngliàng		total amount
5	药品	yàopǐn	*n.*	medicine
6	例如	lìrú	*v.*	take for example
7	比	bǐ	*v.*	to (be the ratio of)
8	过硫酸氢钾	guòliúsuānqīngjiǎ		Potassium peroxymonosulfate
9	溶液	róngyè	*n.*	solution
10	毫升	háoshēng	*measure word*	milliliter (mL)
11	需要	xūyào	*v.*	need
12	克	kè	*measure word*	gram (g)
13	百分之	bǎi fēnzhī		percent (%)
14	烧碱	shāojiǎn	*n.*	Caustic soda

词语练习 Words Exercises

1. 将中文词语和对应的拼音及英文连线。**Match the Chinese words with corresponding *pinyin* and English words.**

1 用量	pèizhì	milliliter (mL)
2 毫升	kè	prepare
3 克	yòngliàng	dosage; amount
4 配制	háoshēng	gram (g)

2. 词语搭配连线。**Match the words.**

1 计算	溶液
2 按照	用量
3 配制	比例
4 组装	设备

学习课文 Text 14-2

Jìsuàn yòngliàng
计算用量

Ànzhào pèizhì xiāodúyè de bǐlì hé zǒngliàng, jìsuàn shuǐ hé xiāodú yàopǐn de yòngliàng. Lìrú, pèizhì yī bǐ èrbǎi de guòliúsuānqīngjiǎ róngyè yìqiān háoshēng, xūyào wǔ kè guòliúsuānqīngjiǎ hé yìqiān háoshēngshuǐ; Pèizhì bǎi fēnzhī sān

按照配制消毒液的比例和总量，计算水和消毒药品的用量。例如，配制 1 比 200（1∶200）的过硫酸氢钾（KHSO5）溶液 1000 毫升，需要 5 克过硫酸氢钾和 1000 毫升水；配制百分之三（3%）

de shāojiǎn róngyè yìqiān háoshēng, xūyào sānshí kè
的烧碱（NaOH）溶液 1000 毫升，需要 30 克
shāojiǎn hé yìqiān háoshēng shuǐ.
烧碱和 1000 毫升水。

Calculating the Amount

Calculate the amount of water and disinfectant medicine, according to the proportion and total amount of the disinfectant solution. For example: Preparing 1000 milliliters of Potassium peroxymonosulfate (KHSO5) solution in the ratio of 1 to 200 requires 5 grams of Potassium peroxymonosulfate and 1000 milliliters of water. Preparing 1000 milliliters of 3% Caustic soda (NaOH) solution, requires 30 grams of Caustic soda and 1000 milliliters of water.

课文练习 Text Exercises

1. 选词填空。Fill in the blanks with the correct words.

A 比例　　B 需要　　C 百分之三　　D 计算

1 配制消毒液需要注意________和总量。

2 配制________（3%）的烧碱溶液。

3 ________30 克烧碱和 1000 毫升水。

4 ________水和消毒药品的用量。

2. 判断正误。True or false.

1 要按照消毒液的比例和总量配制消毒液。

2 配制消毒液需要先计算水和消毒用品的用量。

3 配制 1∶20 的过硫酸氢钾溶液 1000 毫升，需要 10 克过硫酸氢钾和 1000 毫升水。

4 配制 3% 的烧碱溶液 1000 毫升，需要 30 克烧碱和 1000 毫升水。

学习语法 Grammar

语法点 1 Grammar Point 1

万以内数的表达　Expression of numbers up to ten thousand

数字	汉字的写法	汉语的读法
1001	一千零一	yìqiān líng yī
2012	两千零一十二	liǎngqiān líng yīshí'èr
3222	三千两百二十二	sānqiān liǎngbǎi èrshí'èr
4067	四千零六十七	sìqiān líng liùshíqī
9999	九千九百九十九	jiǔqiān jiǔbǎi jiǔshíjiǔ

注意 Notes:

① 整数中间有多个“0”时，只读一个“0”。When there are multiple “0” in the middle of an integer, only one “0” should be read.

② 在位数词“千、百”前，“二、两”都可以出现，在位数词“十”前，只能用“二”。Before the digit words “百”“千”, “二” or “两”can be used to express “two”, before the digit word “十”, only “二” can be used to express “two”.

语法练习 1 Grammar Exercise 1

朗读词语。Read the words aloud.

1	1	5	7	9
2	10	34	59	82
3	112	506	867	910
4	1000	2305	6009	10000

语法点 2 Grammar Point 2

百分数和比例 Percent and ratio

数字	汉字的写法	汉语的读法
3%	百分之三	bǎi fēnzhī sān
100%	百分之百	bǎi fēnzhī bǎi
1 : 200	一比二百	yī bǐ èrbǎi
3 : 2	三比二	sān bǐ èr

例句：

1. Pèizhì yī bǐ èrbǎi de guòliúsuānqīngjiǎ róngyè.
配制1比200的过硫酸氢钾溶液。Prepare a Potassium peroxymonosulfate solution in the ratio of 1 to 200.

2. Pèizhì bǎi fēnzhī sān de shāojiǎn róngyè.
配制 3% 的烧碱溶液。Prepare a 3% Caustic soda solution.

3. Wǒmen gōngsī bǎi fēnzhī bǎi de yǎngzhíchǎng dōu yǒu yǎng jī.
我们公司百分之百的养殖场都有养鸡。All (100%) of our company's livestock and poultry farms raise chickens.

语法练习 2 Grammar Exercise 2

将中文与正确的数字连线。**Match the Chinese to the correct numbers.**

1	百分之三十一	10%
2	1 比 200	3%
3	百分之十	1 : 200
4	百分之三	31%

汉字书写 Writing Chinese Characters

dāo 刀 (刀 刀)

刀 刀 刀 刀 刀

lì 力 (力 力)

力 力 力 力 力

rèn 刃 刃 刃

刃	刃	刃	刃	刃						

wéi 为 为 为 为

为	为	为	为	为						

文化拓展 Culture Insight

The Metric System in China

The metric system in China has a long history, originating from ancient agricultural society and primarily used to measure physical quantities such as length, volume, and weight. During the Xia, Shang, and Zhou dynasties, China had already established relatively unified tools and systems for measuring time, length, capacity, and weight. However, with the development of commodity economy, measurement became a crucial aspect of trade, but the inconsistency and confusion of measurement systems among different regions created problems. After unifying the six kingdoms, Emperor Qin Shihuang issued an imperial edict to standardize measurement and produced a large number of measuring tools which were distributed throughout the country as the standard for measurement. This initiative laid the foundation for the metric system of China's feudal society for over 2,000 years.

小结 Summary

词语 Words

朗读词语。Read the words aloud.

计算	用量	配制	总量	药品
例如	溶液	毫升	需要	

语法 Grammar

语言点回顾。Language points review.

语言点	例
万以内数的表达	1001　一千零一 9999　九千九百九十九
百分数和比例	3%　百分之三 3∶2　三比二

课文理解 Text Comprehension

根据提示复述课文。Retell the text according to the prompts.

按照配制消毒液的________和总量，计算________和消毒药品的用量。例如，配制1∶200的过硫酸氢钾溶液1000毫升，需要________过硫酸氢钾和________水；配制3%的烧碱溶液1000毫升，需要________烧碱和________水。

第15课 Lesson 15

Chēngliáng yàopǐn
称量药品
Weighing the Medicine

复习 Revision

朗读词语。Read the words aloud.

1 yī 一	2 èr 二	3 sān 三	4 sì 四
5 wǔ 五	6 liù 六	7 qī 七	8 bā 八
9 jiǔ 九	10 shí 十	11 shíyī 十一	102 yìbǎi líng èr 一百零二
2050 liǎngqiān líng wǔshí 两千零五十	60% bǎi fēnzhī liùshí 百分之六十	3:5 sān bǐ wǔ 三比五	1:100 yī bǐ yībǎi 一比一百

热身 Warming Up

看图选词。Look at the pictures and choose the correct words.

A 屏幕 (píngmù) screen	B 托盘 (tuōpán) tray
C 勺子 (sháozi) spoon	D 天平 (tiānpíng) balance

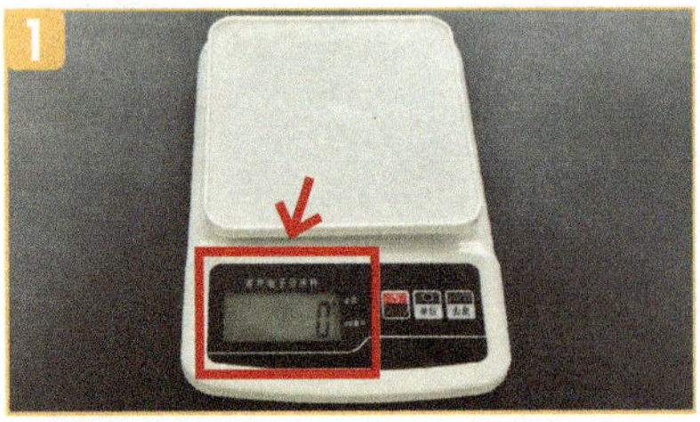

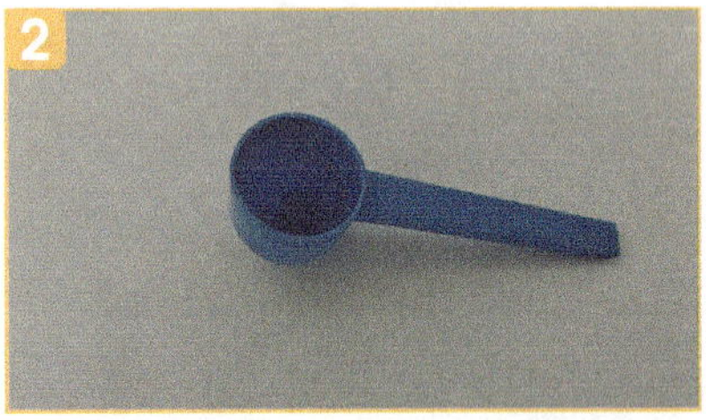

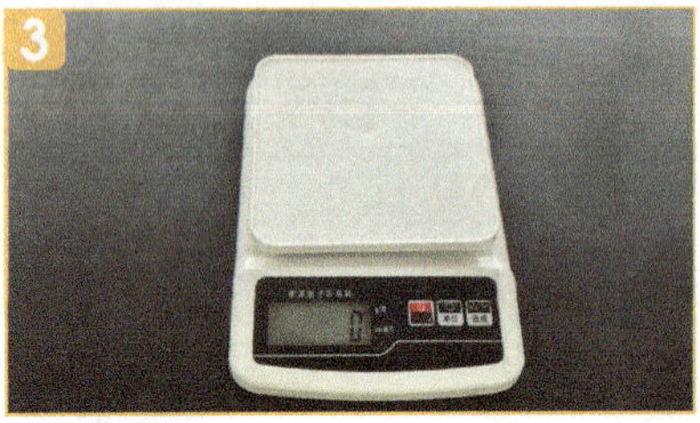

学习生词 Words and Expressions 15-1

1	称量	chēngliáng		weigh
2	把	bǎ	*prep.*	*used to advance the object of a verb to the position before it*

3	天平	tiānpíng	*n.*	balance
4	水平	shuǐpíng	*adj.*	horizontal; level
5	桌面	zhuōmiàn	*n.*	tabletop
6	开机	kāijī	*v.*	power on; start
7	键	jiàn	*n.*	button; key
8	屏幕	píngmù	*n.*	screen
9	显示	xiǎnshì	*v.*	show; display
10	纸	zhǐ	*n.*	paper
11	托盘	tuōpán	*n.*	tray
12	去皮	qùpí		tare; get the net weight
13	勺子	sháozi	*n.*	spoon
14	取	qǔ	*v.*	take; get
15	结束	jiéshù	*v.*	end; finish
16	关机	guānjī	*v.*	power off

词语练习 Words Exercises

1. 将中文词语和对应的拼音及英文连线。**Match the Chinese words with corresponding *pinyin* and English words.**

1 称量 •	• kāijī •	• power on; start
2 开机 •	• guānjī •	• take; get
3 关机 •	• chēngliáng •	• weigh
4 取 •	• qǔ •	• power off

2. 词语分类。Categorize the words.

A 称量	B 把	C 天平	D 水平	E 桌面	F 称量纸
G 键	H 屏幕	I 显示	J 水平	K 托盘	L 去皮
M 勺子	N 取	O 结束	P 关机		

药品称量工具的词语（words for weighing medicine）：

______

学习课文 Text 15-2

Chēngliáng yàopǐn
称量 药品

Yòng tiānpíng chēngliáng wǔ kè yàopǐn de bùzhòu shì:
用天平称量5克药品的步骤是：

Bǎ tiānpíng fàng zài shuǐpíng de zhuōmiàn shang, àn "kāijī" (ON / OFF) jiàn.
把天平放在水平的桌面上，按“开机”（ON / OFF）键。

Píngmù xiǎnshì "líng" hòu, bǎ chēngliángzhǐ fàng zài tuōpán shang, àn "qùpí" jiàn.
屏幕显示“0”后，把称量纸放在托盘上，按“去皮”键。

Píngmù zài xiǎnshì "líng" hòu, yòng sháozi qǔ yàopǐn.
屏幕再显示“0”后，用勺子取药品。

Bǎ yàopǐn fàng zài chēngliángzhǐ shang, chēngliáng wǔ kè yàopǐn.
把药品放在称量纸上，称量5克药品。

Chēngliáng jiéshù hòu, àn "guānjī" (ON / OFF) jiàn, guānjī.
称量结束后，按"关机"（ON / OFF）键，关机。

Weighing the Medicine

Here is the procedure of weighing five grams of medicine with a balance: Place the balance on a table with a horizontal surface and press the "ON / OFF" button. Once the display shows zeros, place the weighing paper on the tray and press the "Tare" button. When the display returns to zero again, use a spoon to take medicine onto the weighing paper until the scale indicates five grams. Once you have the desired amount, press the "ON / OFF" button to power off the balance.

课文练习 Text Exercises

1. 选词填空。Fill in the blanks with the correct words.

A 显示	B 关机	C 称量	D 水平

1. 屏幕________"0"后，把称量纸放在托盘上，按"去皮"键。
2. 用天平________5 克药品。
3. 把天平放在________的桌面上。
4. 称量结束后，按"________"键。

2. 判断正误。True or false.

1 可以用天平称量药品。

2 把称量纸放在托盘上，不需要“去皮”。

3 可以用手取药品。

4 先把天平放在水平的桌面上，再按“开机”键。

学习语法 Grammar

语法点 1 Grammar Point 1

特殊句型：“把”字句（1） Special sentence pattern: the 把 -sentence (1)

“把+宾语+动词+在+处所”形式的“把”字句表示通过对“把”的宾语施加动作，使之产生位置移动。

It is a sentence that indicates the verb imposes an action on the object of “把”, resulting in a change of location for the object.

常用结构：主语 + 把 + 宾语 + 动词 + 在 + 处所

Common structure: subject + 把 + object + verb + 在 + location

例句：

1 Yuángōng bǎ tiānpíng fàng zài shuǐpíng de zhuōmiàn shang.
员工把天平放在水平的桌面上。The employee placed the balance on a table with a horizontal surface.

2 Sìyǎngyuán bǎ gōngzuòfú fàng zài nèi gēngyīshì li.
饲养员把工作服放在内更衣室里。The animal keeper put his/her work clothes in the inner locker room.

3 Dàwèi bǎ shuǐ sǎ zài nán qīnglǐ de wūwù shang.
大卫把水洒在难清理的污物上。David splashed water on the hard-to-clean dirt.

语法练习 1 Grammar Exercise 1

把“把”放在句中合适的位置。**Put “把” in the right place of the sentence.**

1. 大卫____天平放在____水平的桌面上。
2. 员工____药品____放在称量纸上。
3. 员工____称量好的药品____放在消毒桶里。
4. 我们____橡胶手套____戴在手上。

语法点 2 Grammar Point 2

频率、重复副词：再 Adverb of frequency or repetition: 再

频率副词“再”意思是又一次，用在动词的前面，表示同一动作或状态在将来的重复或继续。

The frequency adverb “再” means “once again” and is used before a verb. It indicates the repetition of an action or the continuation of a state in the future.

常用结构：主语 + 再 + 动词性短语

Common structure: subject + 再 + verb phrase

例句：

1. Xiǎnshìqì zài xiǎnshì “líng” hòu, yòng sháozi qǔ yàopǐn.
   显示器再显示“0”后，用勺子取药品。After the display returns to zero again, use a spoon to take the medicine.
2. Sìyǎngyuán chū yǎngzhíchǎng qián yào zài xiāodú suíshēn wùpǐn.
   饲养员出养殖场前要再消毒随身物品。Before exiting the farm, the animal keeper needs to disinfect the belongings with him/her again.
3. Qǐng zài dú yí biàn.
   请再读一遍。Read again, please.

语法练习 2 Grammar Exercise 2

把“再”放在句中合适的位置。Put “再” in the right place of the sentence.

1. ____屏幕____显示“0”后，用勺子取药品。
2. ____出养殖场要____消毒手机等随身物品。
3. ____你在喷洒消毒液前，要____检查圈舍的温度（temperature）和湿度（humidity）。
4. ____明天____来养殖场。

汉字书写 Writing Chinese Characters

nǚ 女 女 女

女 女 女 女 女

zì 字 字 字 字 字 字

字 字 字 字 字

hǎo 好 好 好 好 好 好

好 好 好 好 好

xìng 姓 姓 姓 姓 姓 姓 姓 姓

姓 姓 姓 姓 姓

职业拓展 Career Insight

The Three No's Principle

When using a balance to weigh chemicals, it is indeed necessary to strictly adhere to the "The Three No's Principle", namely not smelling, not touching, and not tasting. These principles aim to ensure the safety and accuracy of experimental operations.

Not smelling: This refers to not sniffing chemicals directly. Many chemical substances have unique odors, and some are even toxic. It is unsafe to identify chemicals through smell, as some toxic gases may enter the body through breathing and cause harm. Therefore, during the experiment, it is essential to avoid sniffing the odor of chemicals directly.

Not touching: This means not touching chemicals directly with one's hands. Most chemical substances are corrosive or irritating, and direct contact with the skin may lead to skin damage or other health issues. Therefore, when using a balance to weigh chemicals, it is recommended to use a spatula or other appropriate tools to avoid direct contact with the chemicals.

Not tasting: This refers to not attempting to taste the chemicals. Chemical substances often have strong flavors, and some are even toxic. Tasting chemicals is an extremely dangerous behavior that can lead to poisoning or other serious consequences. Therefore, during the process of weighing chemicals, it is strictly prohibited to taste any chemicals.

小结 Summary

词语 Words

朗读词语。Read the words aloud.

称量	天平	桌面	开机
屏幕	显示	纸	托盘
句子	结束	关机	

语法 Grammar

语言点回顾。Language points review.

语言点	常用结构	例句
"把"字句（1）：主语＋把＋宾语＋动词＋在＋处所	S＋把＋O＋V+在＋L	员工把天平放在水平的桌面上。 饲养员把工作服放在内更衣室里。
频率、重复副词：再	S＋再＋VP	显示器再显示"0"后，用勺子取药品。 请再读一遍。

课文理解 Text Comprehension

根据提示复述课文。Retell the text according to the prompts.

用天平称量 5 克药品的步骤是：

把天平放在________的桌面上，按“开机”（ON / OFF）键。屏幕显示“0”后，把________放在________上，按“去皮”键。

屏幕再显示“0”后，用________取药品。把药品放在称量纸上，称量 5 克药品。

称量结束后，按“关机”（ON / OFF）键，________。

第16课 Lesson 16

Liángqǔ yòngshuǐ

量取用水

Measuring the Water

复习 Revision

根据提示用"把……放在"完成句子。Complete the sentences with "把……放在" according to the prompts.

1 天平 桌子

____

2 称量纸 天平

____

3 药品 称量纸

____

热身 Warming Up

看图选词。**Look at the pictures and choose the correct words.**

A 量筒 (liángtǒng) measuring cylinder	B 刻度线 (kèdùxiàn) scale mark
C 眼睛 (yǎnjing) eye	D 水面 (shuǐmiàn) surface of water

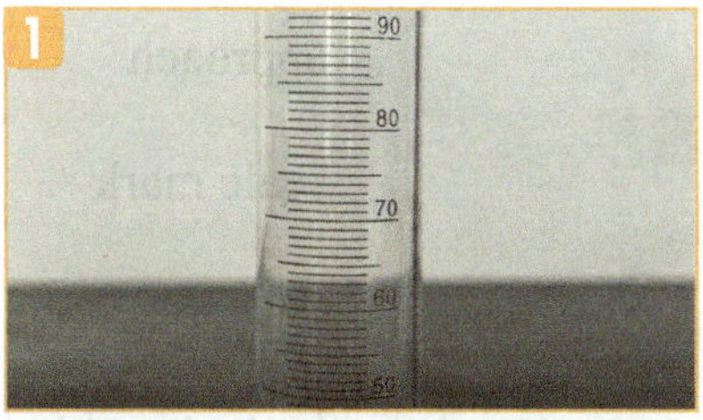

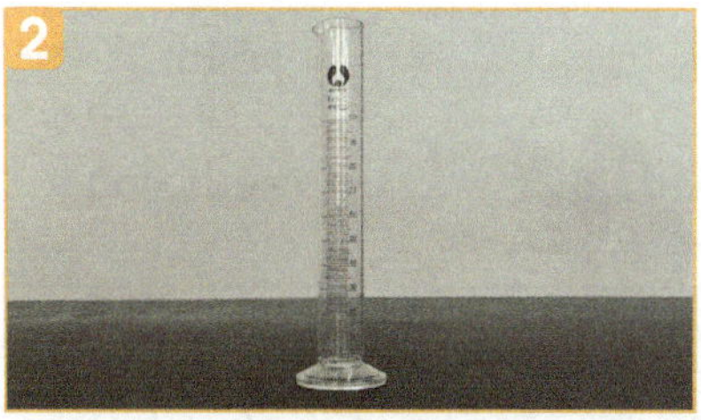

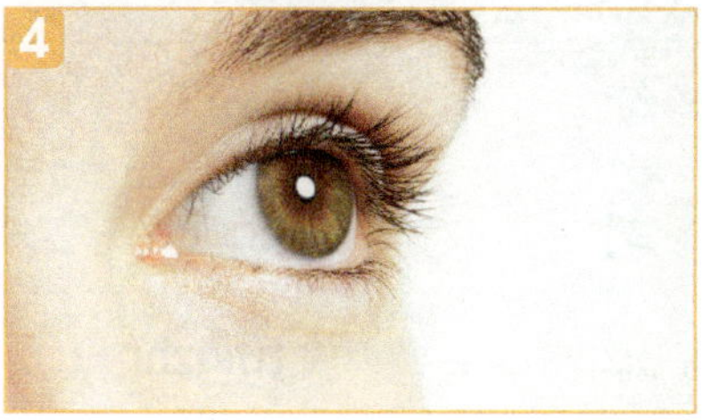

学习生词 Words and Expressions 16-1

1	量取	liángqǔ		measure
2	用水	yòngshuǐ		water (for use)
3	量筒	liángtǒng	*n.*	measuring cylinder

4	适量	shìliàng	*adj.*	appropriate amount
5	缓慢	huǎnmàn	*adj*	slow
6	倒入	dàorù		pull into
7	倒	dào	*v.*	pull
8	（当）……的时候	(dāng)... de shíhou		when..; as...
9	水面	shuǐmiàn	*n.*	surface of water
10	接近	jiējìn	*v.*	approach
11	刻度线	kèdùxiàn		scale mark
12	眼睛	yǎnjing	*n.*	eye
13	平视	píngshì	*v.*	look straight ahead
14	最低处	zuìdīchù		the lowest point
15	继续	jìxù	*v.*	go on; continue
16	达到	dádào	*v.*	achieve
17	停止	tíngzhǐ	*v.*	stop

词语练习 Words Exercises

1. 将中文词语和对应的拼音及英文连线。**Match the Chinese words with corresponding *pinyin* and English words.**

1	量取	tíngzhǐ	look straight ahead
2	倒入	píngshì	stop
3	平视	dàorù	pull into
4	停止	liángqǔ	measure

2. 词语搭配连线。Match the words.

1 准备 •	• 刻度线
2 量取 •	• 工具
3 接近 •	• 用水
4 停止 •	• 倒水

学习课文 Text 16-2

Liángqǔ yòngshuǐ
量取用水

Yòng liángtǒng liángqǔ yìqiān háoshēng shuǐ de fāngfǎ:
用量筒量取1000毫升水的方法：

Xiān bǎ liángtǒng fàng zài shuǐpíng de zhuōmiàn shang, ránhòu zhǔnbèi shìliàng de shuǐ, huǎnmàn dàorù liángtǒng.
先把量筒放在水平的桌面上，然后准备适量的水，缓慢倒入量筒。

Dāng shuǐmiàn jiējìn yìqiān háoshēng kèdùxiàn de shíhou, yǎnjing píngshì shuǐmiàn zuì dī chù, jìxù huǎnmàn dàoshuǐ.
当水面接近1000毫升刻度线的时候，眼睛平视水面最低处，继续缓慢倒水。

Zuìhòu dāng shuǐmiàn zuì dī chù dádào yìqiān háoshēng kèdùxiàn de shíhou, tíngzhǐ dàoshuǐ.
最后当水面最低处达到1000毫升刻度线的时候，停止倒水。

Measuring the Water

Take one thousand milliliters of water with a measuring cylinder.

First, place the measuring cylinder on a table with a horizontal surface. Then, prepare an appropriate amount of water and slowly pour it into the measuring cylinder.

When the water level is close to the 1000 milliliters scale mark, look straight down at the water level at eye level and continue to pour water slowly.

Finally, when the water level reaches the 1000 milliliters scale mark, stop pouring water.

课文练习 Text Exercises

1. 选词填空。Fill in the blanks with the correct words.

A 倒入　　B 平视　　C 适量　　D 停止

1 当水面最低处达到1000毫升刻度线的时候，________倒水。

2 准备________的水。

3 缓慢________量筒。

4 当水面接近1000毫升刻度线的时候，眼睛________水面最低处。

2. 根据课文内容给下列说法排序。Put the statements in the correct order according to the text.

1 当水面接近 1000 毫升刻度线的时候，眼睛平视水面最低处，继续缓慢倒水。

2 首先把量筒放在水平桌面上，然后准备适量的水，缓慢倒入量筒。

3 最后当水面最低处达到 1000 毫升刻度线的时候，停止倒水。

4 用量筒量取 1000 毫升水的方法：

____

学习语法 Grammar

语法点 1 Grammar Point 1

（当）……的时候　when...; as...

“（当）……的时候”多用在句首，表示事件发生的时间点。它前面可以是名词、动词、形容词、数量短语或句子等。

It is commonly placed at the beginning of a sentence to indicate the time point when an event occurs. It can be preceded by nouns, verbs, adjectives, numeral phrases, or clauses.

常用结构：（当）（+ 主语 1）+ 动词性短语 + 的时候，（主语 1+）动词性短语

Common structure: (当) (+ subject 1) + verb phrase + 的时候, (subject 1+) verb phrase

---

例句：1 Dāng shuǐmiàn zuì dī chù dádào yìqiān háoshēng kèdùxiàn de shíhou, tíngzhǐ dào shuǐ.

当水面最低处达到1000毫升刻度线的时候，停止倒水。When the water level reaches the 1000 milliliters scale mark, stop pouring water.

Dāng shuǐmiàn jiējìn yìqiān háoshēng kèdùxiàn de shíhou, yǎnjing píngshì shuǐmiàn zuì dī chù.

2 当水面接近1000毫升刻度线的时候，眼睛平视水面最低处。When the water level is close to the 1000 milliliters scale mark, look straight down at the water level at eye level.

Pēnsǎ pàomò qīngjiéjì de shíhou, yào chuānhǎo yǔyī, yǔkù, jiāoxié.

3 喷洒泡沫清洁剂的时候，要穿好雨衣、雨裤、胶鞋。When spraying foam cleaner, you should wear a raincoat, rain pants, and rubber shoes.

语法练习 1 Grammar Exercise 1

把"（当）……的时候"放在句中合适的位置。Put "（当）……的时候" in the right place of the sentence.

1 ________水面________接近1000毫升刻度线________，眼睛平视水面最低处。

2 ________水面最低处达到1000毫升刻度线________，停止________倒水。

3 ________进入养殖场________，要先洗澡________。

4 ________使用高压水枪________，一只手________握高压水枪把手，另一只手握高压水枪的中间位置。

语法点 2 Grammar Point 2

程度副词：最　Adverb of degree: 最

"最"用在形容词前，表示在同类事物中，某种事物性质或心理活动超过其他，达到顶点。

The adverb " 最 " is used before adjectives to signify that among similar things, a certain thing's nature or psychological state surpass all others, reaching a peak or the utmost degree.

常用结构：最 + 形容词 + 名词

Common structure: 最 + adjective + noun

例句：

1. Zuì dī chù.
最低处。The lowest point.

2. Zuì nán qīnglǐ de wūwù.
最难清理的污物。The hardest-to-clean dirt.

3. Zuì dà de shuǐtǒng.
最大的水桶。The largest water bucket.

语法练习 2 Grammar Exercise 2

按照正确的语序连词成句。Make sentences in correct orders with the given words or phrases.

1. ①水面 ②最 ③低 ④处

____

2. ①最 ②难清理 ③污物 ④的

____

3. ①最 ②要 ③后 ④关闭电源

____

4. ①大 ②最 ③的 ④养殖场

____

汉字书写 Writing Chinese Characters

yòu 又 又

又	又	又	又	又						

shuāng 双 双 双 双

双	双	双	双	双						

duì 对 对 对 对 对

对	对	对	对	对						

yǒu 友 友 友 友

友	友	友	友	友						

文化拓展 Culture Insight

Compendium of Materia Medica

The *Compendium of Materia Medica* is a monumental medical work compiled by the renowned pharmacist Li Shizhen of the Ming Dynasty. In this book, Li Shizhen offers detailed explanations of the properties, primary uses, and prescribing rules of each medicine, providing invaluable references for successive generations of medical practitioners. Even Charles Darwin, the founder of the theory of evolution in the United Kingdom, acclaimed *Compendium of Materia Medica* as an "ancient Chinese encyclopedia", demonstrating the profound influence of Li Shizhen and his work. It is evident that the impact of Li Shizhen and his *Compendium of Materia Medica* is indeed significant.

小结 Summary

词语 Words

朗读词语。Read the words aloud.

量筒	适量	缓慢	水面
接近	刻度线	眼睛	平视
继续	停止		

语法 Grammar

语言点回顾。Language points review.

语言点	常用结构	例句
（当）……的时候	（当）（+ S_1）+ VP + 的时候，（S_1+）VP	当水面最低处达到 1000 毫升刻度线的时候，停止倒水。 当水面接近 1000 毫升刻度线的时候，眼睛平视水面最低处。
程度副词：最	最 + Adj + N	最低处。 最难清理的污物。

课文理解 Text Comprehension

根据提示复述课文。Retell the text according to the prompts.

用量筒量取 1000 毫升水的方法：

先把量筒放在________桌面上，然后准备________的水，________倒入量筒。

当水面接近 1000 毫升________的时候，眼睛________水面最低处，继续缓慢倒水。

最后当水面________达到 1000 毫升刻度线的时候，________倒水。

第17课
Lesson 17

Pēnsǎ zhǔnbèi
喷洒准备
Preparation for Spraying

复习 Revision

朗读句子。Read the sentences aloud.

1 先把量筒放在水平桌面上，然后准备适量的水，缓慢倒入量筒。

2 当水面接近 1000 毫升刻度线的时候，眼睛平视水面最低处，继续缓慢倒水。

3 最后当水面最低处达到 1000 毫升刻度线的时候，停止倒水。

热身 Warming Up

认读词语。Learn and read the words.

1 shīdù 湿度 humidity

2 wēndù 温度 temperature

3 pēnwù 喷雾 spray

4 héshì 合适 appropriate; suitable

5 quèbǎo 确保 ensure

6 zhèngcháng 正常 normal

学习生词 Words and Expressions 17-1

1	检查	jiǎnchá	*v.*	check
2	温度	wēndù	*n.*	temperature
3	湿度	shīdù	*n.*	humidity
4	合适	héshì	*adj.*	appropriate; suitable
5	摄氏度	shèshìdù	*measure word*	degree Celsius (℃)
6	左右	zuǒyòu	*n.*	(used after a number) about; around
7	确保	quèbǎo	*v.*	ensure
8	喷雾	pēnwù		spray; atomize
9	正常	zhèngcháng	*adj.*	normal
10	漏	lòu	*v.*	leak
11	气	qì	*n.*	air; gas

词语练习 Words Exercises

1. 将中文词语和对应的拼音及英文连线。Match the Chinese words with corresponding *pinyin* and English words.

1 合适 •	• zuǒyòu •	• normal
2 检查 •	• héshì •	• appropriate; suitable
3 正常 •	• jiǎnchá •	• about; around
4 左右 •	• zhèngcháng •	• check

2. 词语搭配连线。**Match the words.**

1 检查 •	• 气
	• 温度
2 漏 •	• 水
	• 湿度

学习课文 Text 17-2

Pēnsǎ zhǔnbèi
喷洒准备

Pēnsǎ xiāodúyè qián, jiǎnchá juànshè de wēndù hé shīdù.
喷洒消毒液前，检查圈舍的温度和湿度。Héshì de wēndù shì èrshí shèshìdù zuǒyòu, héshì de shīdù shì bǎi fēnzhī liùshíwǔ zuǒyòu.
合适的温度是 20 摄氏度（℃）左右，合适的湿度是 65% 左右。

Zhǔnbèi hǎo pēnsǎ shèbèi, quèbǎo pēnwù zhèngcháng, gègè jiēkǒu bú lòu qì, bú lòu shuǐ.
准备好喷洒设备，确保喷雾正常，各个接口不漏气、不漏水。

Preparation for Spraying

Before spraying disinfectant, check the temperature and humidity in the animal pens. The appropriate temperature should be around 20 degrees Celsius, while the appropriate humidity should be around 65%.

Prepare the spraying equipment and ensure that the spray functions properly and all the connectors are leak-free, both for air and water.

课文练习 Text Exercises

1. 选词填空。Fill in the blanks with the correct words.

A 检查	B 湿度	C 温度	D 确保

1 准备好喷洒设备，________喷雾正常。

2 喷洒消毒液前，________圈舍的温度和湿度。

3 合适的________是 20℃ 左右，合适________的是 65% 左右。

2. 根据课文内容给下列说法排序。Put the statements in the correct order according to the text.

1 确保各个接口不漏气、不漏水。

2 喷洒消毒液前，检查圈舍的温度和湿度。

3 准备好喷洒设备。

____

学习语法 Grammar

语法点 1 Grammar Point 1

概数表示法：左右 Expression of approximate number: 左右

概数表示比某一数量稍多或稍少。“数量短语 + 左右”是概数的一种表示形式。

An approximate number indicates a quantity that is slightly more or less than a specific number. One way to express an approximate number in Chinese is “Numeral phrase + 左右”.

常用结构：数量短语 + 左右

Common structure: numeral phrase + 左右

例句：

1. Liù zhī zuǒyòu.
   6 只左右。Around 6.
2. èrshí shèshìdù zuǒyòu.
   20℃ 左右。Around 20 degrees Celsius.
3. Wǔ ge rén zuǒyòu.
   5 个人左右。About 5 people.

语法练习 1 Grammar Exercise 1

判断正误。True or false.

1. 6 只左右鸡。
2. 3 个人左右。
3. 温度是 20℃ 左右。
4. 湿度是左右 55%。

语法点 2 Grammar Point 2

否定副词：不 Adverb of negation：不

汉语对动作行为或性质表示否定一般用副词“不”加在动词或形容词前面。“有”的否定用“没”，不用“不”。

In Chinese, negation of actions, behaviors, or properties is generally expressed by adding the adverb “不” before a verb or adjective. The negation of “有” is “没”, not “不”.

常用结构：不 + 动词性短语 / 形容词

Common structure: 不 + verb phrase / adjective

例句：

1. Bú lòu qì. 不漏气。It doesn’t leak air.
2. Bù hǎo. 不好。Not good.
3. Wǒ bú jiào Dàwèi. 我不叫大卫。My name is not David.

语法练习 2 Grammar Exercise 2

用“不”或“没有”改写句子。Rewrite the sentences with “不” or “没有”.

1. 我认识大卫。
____
2. 他是中国人。
____
3. 我叫大卫。
____
4. 我有钱（money）。
____

汉字书写 Writing Chinese Characters

shuǐ 水 水 水 水

水	水	水	水	水						

huǒ 火 火 火 火

火	火	火	火	火						

yún 云 云 云 云

云	云	云	云	云						

shān 山 山 山

山	山	山	山	山						

职业拓展 Career Insight

Preparing the Disinfectant with Clean Water

When preparing disinfectant, the water must be clean, such as tap water, but it should not be unfiltered water from rivers, streams, lakes, ponds or other sources. This is because these waters contain more impurities, which can easily block the nozzle. Additionally, the complex composition of these waters can react with disinfectants, thereby affecting the disinfection effect.

小结 Summary

词语 Words

朗读词语。Read the words aloud.

检查	温度	湿度	合适
摄氏度	左右	确保	喷雾
正常	漏	气	

语法 Grammar

语言点回顾。Language points review.

语言点	常用结构	例句
概数表示法：左右	NumP + 左右	20℃左右。 5 个人左右。
否定副词：不	不 + VP / Adj	不漏气。 不好。

课文理解 Text Comprehension

根据提示复述课文。Retell the text according to the prompts.

喷洒消毒液前，检查圈舍的________和________。合适的温度是________左右，合适的湿度是________左右。准备好喷洒设备，确保喷雾________，各个接口不________、不________。

第18课 Lesson 18

Pēnsǎ xiāodúyè
喷洒消毒液
Spraying the Disinfectant

复习 Revision

根据课文内容回答问题。**Answer the questions according to the text.**

1. 喷洒消毒液前，需要检查圈舍的温度和湿度吗？
2. 喷洒消毒液前，需要检查喷雾设备吗？
3. 喷洒消毒液的时候，圈舍合适的温度是多少？
4. 喷洒消毒液的时候，圈舍合适的湿度是多少？

热身 Warming Up

认读词语。**Learn and read the words.**

1. shuǐwèixiàn 水位线 water line
2. biǎomiàn 表面 surface
3. suǒyǒu 所有 all
4. xiǎoshí 小时 hour
5. wùtǐ 物体 object
6. qūyù 区域 area

学习生词 Words and Expressions 18-1

1	能	néng	*v.*	can
2	超过	chāoguò	*v.*	exceed
3	最	zuì	*adv.*	most
4	高	gāo	*adj.*	high; tall
5	水位线	shuǐwèixiàn		water line
6	覆盖	fùgài	*v.*	cover
7	所有	suǒyǒu	*adj.*	all
8	物体	wùtǐ	*n.*	object
9	表面	biǎomiàn	*n.*	surface
10	两	liǎng	*num.*	two; a couple of
11	小时	xiǎoshí	*n.*	hour
12	区域	qūyù	*n.*	area

词语练习 Words Exercises

1. 将中文词语和对应的拼音及英文连线。**Match the Chinese words with corresponding *pinyin* and English words.**

1 超过 •	• fùgài •	• area
2 物体 •	• chāoguò •	• cover
3 覆盖 •	• wùtǐ •	• object
4 区域 •	• qūyù •	• exceed

2. 词语搭配连线。**Match the words.**

1 最	物体
	高
2 所有	区域
	好

学习课文 Text 18-2

Pēnsǎ xiāodúyè
喷洒消毒液

Bǎ xiāodúyè dào zài pēnwù shèbèi li, zhùyì bù néng chāoguò zuì
把消毒液倒在喷雾设备里，注意不能超过最
gāo shuǐwèixiàn. Zuòhǎo fánghù, shǐyòng pēnwù shèbèi, duìzhǔn wéilán
高水位线。做好防护，使用喷雾设备，对准围栏
děng wèizhi jūnyún pēnsǎ xiāodúyè, quèbǎo xiāodúyè fùgài suǒyǒu
等位置均匀喷洒消毒液，确保消毒液覆盖所有
wùtǐ biǎomiàn. Pēnsǎ jiéshù liǎng ge xiǎoshí hòu, yòng shuǐ chōngxǐ xiāodú
物体表面。喷洒结束两个小时后，用水冲洗消毒
qūyù.
区域。

Spraying the Disinfectant

Pour the disinfectant into the spray equipment, and be

careful not to exceed the highest water line. Get well protected and use spray equipment to evenly spray the disinfectant on places like fences, ensuring that the disinfectant covers the surfaces of all the objects. Two hours after spraying, rinse the disinfected area with clean water.

课文练习 Text Exercises

1. 选词填空。Fill in the blanks with the correct words.

A 冲洗　　B 小时　　C 覆盖　　D 超过　　E 均匀

1 把消毒液倒在喷雾设备里，注意不能________最高水位线。

2 使用喷雾设备，对准围栏等位置________喷洒消毒液。

3 确保消毒液________所有物体表面。

4 喷洒结束两个________后，用水________消毒区域。

2. 根据课文内容给下列说法排序。Put the statements in the correct order according to the text.

1 喷洒结束两个小时后，用水冲洗消毒区域。

2 把消毒液倒在喷雾设备里，注意不能超过最高水位线。

3 确保消毒液覆盖所有物体表面。

4 做好防护，使用喷雾设备，对准围栏等位置均匀喷洒消毒液。

____

学习语法 Grammar

语法点 1 Grammar Point 1

能愿动词：能　Modal verb: 能

能愿动词“能”用在动词的前面，表示有能力、有条件做某事，或者情理上、某种条件下允许做某事。

The modal verb “能” is used before a verb to indicate that one has the ability or conditions to do something, or that it is allowed under certain conditions or circumstances.

常用结构：（1）肯定形式：主语 + 能 + 动词性短语；（2）否定形式：主语 + 不 + 能 + 动词性短语

Common structure: (1) Affirmative form: subject + 能 + verb phrase, (2) Negative form: subject + 不 + 能 + verb phrase

例句：

1. Wǒ néng yòng tiānpíng chēngliáng yàopǐn.
   我能用天平称量药品。I can weigh the medicine with a balance.
2. Tā néng shuō Zhōngwén.
   他能说中文。He can speak Chinese.
3. Xiāodúyè bù néng chāoguò zuì gāo shuǐwèixiàn.
   消毒液不能超过最高水位线。The level of disinfectant should not exceed the highest water line.

语法练习 1 Grammar Exercise 1

把“能”放在句中合适的位置。**Put “能” in the right place of the sentence.**

1. 消毒液____不____超过最高水位线。
2. ____饲养员____进入圈舍。

3 大卫____调节____高压水枪的泡沫清洁剂和水的比例。

4 我们____用紫外线灯消毒____随身物品。

语法点 2 Grammar Point 2

数词：二、两　Numerals: 二 / 两

都表示数字“2”，但用法不一样。

The numerals “ 二 ” and “ 两 ” both represent the number two in Chinese, but they differ in usage.

	两	二
数数、读数字 count and read numbers	×	√
位数词“十”前 before the numeral of “ 十 ”	×	√
位数词“百、千、万、亿”前 before the numeral of “ 百、千、万、亿 ”	√	√
量词前 before the measure word	√	×

常用结构：两 + 百 / 千 / 万 / 亿

Common structure: 两 + 百 / 千 / 万 / 亿 (hundred / thousand / ten thousand / one hundred million)

例句：

1 Pēnsǎ jiéshù liǎng ge xiǎoshí hòu, yòng shuǐ chōngxǐ xiāodú qūyù.
喷洒结束两个小时后，用水冲洗消毒区域。Two hours after spraying, rinse the disinfected area with clean water.

2 Shí'èr wèi yuángōng li, yǒu liǎng wèi shòuyī, shí wèi sìyǎngyuán.
十二位员工里，有两位兽医，十位饲养员。Among the twelve employees, there are two veterinarians and ten animal keepers.

3 Yǎngzhíchǎng li yǒu liǎngbǎi zhī yáng.
养殖场里有两百只羊。There are two hundred sheep in the farm.

语法练习 2 Grammar Exercise 2

选词填空。Fill in the blanks with the correct words.

A 两　　B 二

1. 喷洒结束________个小时后，才能用水冲洗消毒区域。
2. 公司有________十（20）位员工。
3. 圈舍里有________百头牛。
4. 兽医工作了十________（12）天。

汉字书写 Writing Chinese Characters

tóu 头

fā 发

shǒu 手

zú 足

文化拓展 Culture Insight

Intelligent Animal Husbandry

Nowadays, China is applying new information technologies such as the Internet of Things, cloud computing, big data and artificial intelligence to build a smart animal husbandry system, developing knowledge-intensive, technology-driven and modern smart animal husbandry practices, thereby advancing the modernization of animal husbandry.

小结 Summary

词语 Words

朗读词语。Read the words aloud.

能	超过	最	高
水位线	覆盖	所有	物体
表面	两	个	小时
区域			

语法 Grammar

语言点回顾。Language points review.

语言点	常用结构	例句
能愿动词：能	肯定形式：S+ 能 +VP 否定形式：S+ 不 + 能 +VP	我能用天平称量药品。 消毒液不能超过最高水位线。
数词：二、两	两 + 百 / 千 / 万 / 亿	喷洒结束两个小时后，用水冲洗消毒区域。 十二位员工里，有两位兽医，十位饲养员。

课文理解 Text Comprehension

根据提示复述课文。Retell the text according to the prompts.

把消毒液倒在喷雾设备里，注意不能超过________水位线。做好________，使用喷雾设备，对准围栏等位置________喷洒消毒液，确保消毒液覆盖所有物体________。喷洒结束________个小时后，用水________消毒区域。

第19课 Lesson 19

Shǐyòng fēnzǐ xuánfú xiāodújī
使用分子悬浮消毒机
Using the Molecular Suspension Disinfection Machine

复习 Revision

朗读句子。Read the sentences aloud.

1. 把消毒液倒在喷雾设备里，注意不能超过最高水位线。
2. 做好防护，使用喷雾设备。
3. 对准围栏等位置均匀喷洒消毒液，确保消毒液覆盖所有物体表面。
4. 喷洒结束两个小时后，用水冲洗消毒区域。

热身 Warming Up

认读词语。Learn and read the words.

1. gàizi 盖子 lid; cover
2. shíjiān 时间 time

3 菜单 (càidān) menu　　4 安装 (ānzhuāng) install

5 设置 (shèzhì) set up; install　　6 确认 (quèrèn) affirm; confirm

学习生词 Words and Expressions 19-1

1	分子悬浮消毒机	fēnzǐ xuánfú xiāodújī		molecular suspension disinfection machine
2	增效剂	zēngxiàojì		enhancer
3	安装	ānzhuāng	*v.*	install
4	到	dào	*v.*	*used as a verb compliment to indicate the result of an action*
5	盖子	gàizi	*n.*	lid; cover
6	瓶盖	pínggài		bottle cap
7	刷卡	shuākǎ	*v.*	swipe a card
8	菜单	càidān	*n.*	menu
9	秒	miǎo	*measure word*	second
10	参数	cānshù	*n.*	parameter
11	界面	jièmiàn	*n.*	interface
12	设置	shèzhì	*v.*	set up; install
13	时间	shíjiān	*n.*	time
14	确认	quèrèn	*v.*	affirm; confirm
15	开始	kāishǐ	*v.*	start; begin
16	熏蒸	xūnzhēng	*v.*	fumigate

词语练习 Words Exercises

1. 将中文词语和对应的拼音及英文连线。Match the Chinese words with corresponding *pinyin* and English words.

1 增效剂	jièmiàn	menu
2 盖子	càidān	enhancer
3 菜单	zēngxiàojì	lid; cover
4 界面	gàizi	interface

2. 词语搭配连线。Match the words.

1 打开	熏蒸
2 设置	瓶盖
3 进入	参数
4 开始	界面

学习课文 Text 19-2

Shǐyòng fēnzǐ xuánfú xiāodújī
使用分子悬浮消毒机

Bǎ xiāodúyè hé zēngxiàojì ānzhuāng dào xiāodújī shang, nǐngjǐn gàizi.
把消毒液和增效剂安装到消毒机上，拧紧盖子。

Liánjiē diànyuán, bǎ zēngxiàojì pínggài fàngdào shuākǎ qūyù,
连接电源，把增效剂瓶盖放到刷卡区域，

shuākǎ.
刷卡。

Àn “càidān” jiàn wǔ miǎo, jìnrù cānshù tiáojié jièmiàn. Àn
按“菜单”键 5 秒，进入参数调节界面。按

jiàn shèzhì pēnsǎ shíjiān, àn jiàn
“+”“-”键设置喷洒时间，按“ENTER”键

quèrèn.
确认。

Dāng píngmù xiǎnshì de shíhou, ànxia
当屏幕显示“READY”的时候，按下

“kāiguān” jiàn, kāishǐ xūnzhēng xiāodú.
“开关”键，开始熏蒸消毒。

Using the Molecular Suspension Disinfection Machine

Install the disinfectant and enhancer into the disinfection machine and tighten the lid.

Connect the power, and place the cap of the enhancer bottle on the card swiping area, then swipe the card.

Press and hold the “Menu” button for five seconds to enter the parameter adjustment interface. Press the “ + ” and the “ – ” buttons to set the spraying time, and press the “ENTER” button to confirm.

When the display shows “READY”, press the “Power” button to start fumigation and disinfection.

课文练习 Text Exercises

1. 选词填空。Fill in the blanks with the correct words.

A 刷卡　　B 确认　　C 设置　　D 界面

1. 按“ENTER”键________。
2. 把增效剂瓶盖放到________区域。
3. 按“+”“-”键________喷洒时间。
4. 按“菜单键”5 秒，进入参数调节________。

2. 根据课文内容给下列说法排序。Put the statements in the correct order according to the text.

1. 连接电源，把增效剂瓶盖放到刷卡区域，刷卡。
2. 把消毒液和增效剂安装到消毒机上，拧紧盖子。
3. 按“+”“-”键设置喷洒时间，按“ENTER”键确认。
4. 按“菜单”键 5 秒，进入参数调节界面。
5. 当屏幕显示“READY”的时候，按下“开关”键，开始熏蒸消毒。

____

学习语法 Grammar

语法点 1 Grammar Point 1

趋向补语（1）：动词 + 下 Complement of direction (1): verb + 下

趋向补语“下”表示使某物固定下来，如“写下名字、按下开关键”。

The directional complement “ 下 ” indicates making something fixed, for example “ 写下名字 (write down the name)” and “ 按下 ‘ 开关 ’ 键 (press the ‘Power’ button)”.

例句：

1. Qǐng xiěxia nǐ de míngzi.
   请写下你的名字。Please write down your name.
2. Ànxia “kāiguān” jiàn, kāishǐ xūnzhēng xiāodú.
   按下“开关”键，开始熏蒸消毒。Press the “Power” button to start fumigation and disinfection.
3. Ànxia “càidān” jiàn wǔmiǎo, jìnrù cānshù tiáojié jièmiàn.
   按下“菜单”键5秒，进入参数调节界面。Press and hold the “Menu” button for five seconds to enter the parameter adjustment interface.

语法练习 1 Grammar Exercise 1

把“下”放在句中合适的位置。Put “ 下 ” in the right place of the sentence.

1. 请____写____你的名字。
2. 请____按____高压水枪扳机。
3. ____按____“开关”键，开始熏蒸消毒。
4. ____按____“菜单”键，进入参数调节界面。

语法点 2 Grammar Point 2

特殊句型：“把”字句（2） Special sentence pattern: the 把 -sentence (2)

“把＋宾语＋动词＋到＋处所”结构的“把”字句表示通过对宾语施加动作，使之位置移动到达某个处所。

It is a sentence that indicates the action exerted on an object, causing it to move and arrive at a specific location.

常用结构：主语＋把＋宾语＋动词＋到＋处所

Common structure: subject + 把 + object + verb + 到 + location

例句：

1. Wǒ bǎ xiāodúyè hé zēngxiàojì ānzhuāng dào xiāodújī shang.
   我把消毒液和增效剂安装到消毒机上。I installed the disinfectant and enhancer onto the disinfection machine.
2. Dàwèi bǎ xiāodúyè pēnsǎ dào wéilán shang.
   大卫把消毒液喷洒到围栏上。David sprayed the disinfectant onto the fence.
3. Dàwèi bǎ tiānpíng fàngdào shuǐpíng de zhuōmiàn shang.
   大卫把天平放到水平的桌面上。David placed the balance on a table with a horizontal surface.

语法练习 2 Grammar Exercise 2

选词填空。**Fill in the blanks with the correct words.**

A 把　　B 到

1. 他________消毒液和增效剂安装________消毒机上。
2. 我________增效剂瓶盖放________刷卡区域。

3 我们________称量好的药品放________消毒桶里。

4 员工________进水管连接________泵体进水口。

汉字书写 Writing Chinese Characters

mén 门 门 门

门	门	门	门	门						

men 们 们 们 们 们

们	们	们	们	们						

wèn 问 问 问 问 问 问

问	问	问	问	问						

jiān 间 间 间 间 间 间 间

间	间	间	间	间						

职业拓展 Career Insight

Choosing the Appropriate Disinfectant

In livestock and poultry production, the most commonly utilized disinfectants can be roughly divided into alkalis, acids, aldehydes, phenols, quaternary ammonium salts, halogens, oxidants, alcohols and other types according to their chemical composition. They vary in their application concentrations, methods, and targets for disinfection. In actual production, the appropriate disinfectant and its usage can be selected according to specific circumstances for disinfection purposes.

小结 Summary

词语 Words

朗读词语。Read the words aloud.

盖子	刷卡	菜单	秒	参数
界面	设置	时间	确认	开始

语法 Grammar

语言点回顾。Language points review.

语言点	常用结构	例句
趋向补语（1）：V + 下	V + 下	按下菜单键，进入参数调节界面。 按下开关键，开始熏蒸消毒。

（续表）

语言点	常用结构	例句
“把”字句（2）：主语＋把＋宾语＋动词＋到＋处所	S＋把＋O＋V＋到＋L	大卫把消毒液和增效剂安装到消毒机上。 大卫把消毒液喷洒到围栏上。

课文理解 Text Comprehension

根据提示复述课文。Retell the text according to the prompts.

把消毒液和增效剂安装到________上，拧紧________。

连接________，把增效剂瓶盖放到________区域，刷卡。

按“菜单”键 5 秒，进入参数调节________。按“＋”“－”键设置喷洒________，按“ENTER”键________。

当屏幕显示“READY”的时候，按下“________”键，开始熏蒸消毒。

第20课 Lesson 20

Xūnzhēng cāozuò
熏蒸操作
Fumigation Operation

复习 Revision

朗读句子。Read the sentences aloud.

1. 把消毒液喷洒到围栏上。
2. 把天平放到水平的桌面上。
3. 按“开关”键，开始熏蒸消毒。
4. 按“菜单”键，进入参数调节界面。

热身 Warming Up

看图选词。Look at the pictures and choose the correct words.

A 排气扇 (páiqìshàn) exhaust fan	B 门 (mén) door; gate
C 窗 (chuāng) window	D 人 (rén) people; human being

1

2

3

4

学习生词 Words and Expressions 20-1

1	操作	cāozuò	*v.*	operate
2	关	guān	*v.*	close
3	门	mén	*n.*	door; gate
4	窗	chuāng	*n.*	window
5	密封	mìfēng	*v.*	seal up
6	排气扇	páiqìshàn		exhaust fan
7	人	rén	*n.*	people; human being
8	动物	dòngwù	*n.*	animal
9	接下来	jiēxiàlái		next; then
10	通风	tōngfēng	*v.*	ventilate
11	期间	qījiān	*n.*	time; period
12	一定	yídìng	*adv.*	surely; certainly; necessarily

词语练习 Words Exercises

1. 将中文词语和对应的拼音及英文连线。Match the Chinese words with corresponding *pinyin* and English words.

1 关紧	páiqìshàn	exhaust fan
2 通风	mìfēng	seal up
3 排气扇	guānjǐn	ventilate
4 密封	tōngfēng	fasten up

2. 反义词连线。Match the antonyms.

1 打开	密封
2 内	关紧
3 通风	下
4 上	外

学习课文 Text 20-2

Xūnzhēng cāozuò
熏蒸操作

Xūnzhēng xiāodú qián yào guānjǐn mén hé chuāng, mìfēng páiqìshàn, quèbǎo juànshè li bù néng yǒu rén hé dòngwù.
熏蒸消毒前要关紧门和窗，密封排气扇，确保圈舍里不能有人和动物。

Jiēxiàlai, shǐyòng fēnzǐ xuánfú xiāodújī xiāodú 15 fēnzhōng.
接下来，使用分子悬浮消毒机消毒15分钟。

Mìfēng shí'èr dào èrshísì xiǎoshí hòu, dǎkāi chuāng tōngfēng.
密封 12—24 小时后，打开窗通风。
Zhùyì, mìfēng qījiān yídìng bù néng jìnrù juànshè.
注意，密封期间一定不能进入圈舍。

Fumigation Operation

Before fumigation and disinfection, close the doors and windows tightly and seal up the exhaust fans to ensure that no people or animals are present in the animal pens.

Utilize the molecular suspension disinfection machine to disinfect the area for 15 minutes.

Following disinfection, maintain a sealed environment in the animal pens for 12 to 24 hours. After the sealing period, open the windows for ventilation. Pay attention: Do not enter the animal pens during the sealing time.

课文练习 Text Exercises

1. 选词填空。Fill in the blanks with the correct words.

A 密封	B 动物	C 关紧	D 通风

1. 熏蒸消毒前要________门窗，密封排风扇。
2. 熏蒸消毒时，圈舍中不能有人和________。

3 ________期间一定不能开窗，不能进入圈舍。

4 密封 12—24 小时后，开窗________。

2. 根据课文内容给下列说法排序。Put the statements in the correct order according to the text.

1 使用分子悬浮消毒机消毒 15 分钟。

2 开窗通风。

3 密封圈舍 12—24 小时。

4 熏蒸消毒前要关紧门窗，密封排风扇。

____

学习语法 Grammar

语法点 1 Grammar Point 1

特殊句型：“有”字句　Special sentence pattern: the 有 -sentence

表示某个处所存在某些人或事物。

It indicates the presence of certain people or things in a place.

常用结构：（1）肯定形式：处所 + 有 + 名词性短语；（2）否定形式：处所 + 没有 + 名词性短语

Common structure: (1) Affirmative form: location + 有 + noun phrase, (2) Negative form: location + 没有 + noun phrase

例句：

1 Xǐzǎojiān yǒu rén.
洗澡间有人。There is someone in the bathroom.

2 Juànshè yǒu páiqìshàn.
圈舍有排气扇。There are exhaust fans in the animal pens.

3 Pēnhú li méiyǒu shuǐ.
喷壶里没有水。There is no water in the spray bottle.

语法练习 1 Grammar Exercise 1

用“没有”改写句子。Rewrite the sentences with “没有”.

1 更衣室有工作服。

____

2 喷壶里有水。

____

3 圈舍里有鸡。

____

4 洗澡间有人。

____

语法点 2 Grammar Point 2

副词：一定　Adverb: 一定

用在动词前面，通常用于表示肯定或确定的语气，强调某件事情是确定无疑的。用于肯定句中，表示一种强烈的肯定或确认。

It is used before a verb, usually to express a certain or confirmed tone, emphasizing that something is definitely true and undoubted. It is used in positive sentences to express a strong affirmation or confirmation.

常用结构：一定 +（不能）动词性短语

Common structure: 一定 +（不能）verb phrase

例句：

1 Yídìng xiān xǐzǎo, zài jìnrù yǎngzhíchǎng.
一定先洗澡，再进入养殖场。You must take a shower before entering the livestock and poultry farm.

2 Mìfēng qījiān, yídìng bù néng kāi chuāng.
密封期间，一定不能开窗。During the sealing time, the windows must not be opened.

3 Shǐyòng gāoyā shuǐqiāng yídìng yào zhùyì ānquán.
使用高压水枪一定要注意安全。When using a high-pressure water gun, you must pay attention to safety.

语法练习 2 Grammar Exercise 2

把“一定”放在句中合适的位置。Put “一定” in the right place of the sentence.

1. 密封期间____不能____开窗。
2. 密封 12—24 小时后，____要开窗____通风。
3. 进入养殖场前，____要进入更衣室____穿工作服和工作鞋。
4. 喷雾设备里的消毒液，____不能超过____最高水位线。

汉字书写 Writing Chinese Characters

bái 白 白 白 白 白

白 白 白 白 白

de 的 的 的 的 的 的 的 的

的 的 的 的 的

lì 立 立 立 立 立

立 立 立 立 立

wèi 位 位 位 位 位 位 位

位 位 位 位 位

文化拓展 Culture Insight

Chinese Tea Culture

China is the birthplace of tea, where it was discovered and used over 4,700 years ago. Chaozhou Gongfu Tea is a typical representative of Chinese tea art, integrating spirit, etiquette, brewing skills, the art of tea tasting, and quality evaluation. For thousands of years, China has accumulated a large amount of material culture on tea cultivation and production, forming a rich spiritual culture on tea.

小结 Summary

词语 Words

朗读词语。Read the words aloud.

操作	门	窗	密封
人	动物	通风	一定

语法 Grammar

语言点回顾。Language points review.

语言点	常用结构	例句
"有"字句（表存在）	肯定形式：L + 有 + NP 否定形式：L + 没有 + NP	圈舍有排气扇。 圈舍没有排气扇。

（续表）

语言点	常用结构	例句
副词：一定	一定＋（不能）VP	一定先洗澡，再进入养殖场。 密封期间，一定不能开窗。

课文理解 Text Comprehension

根据提示复述课文。Retell the text according to the prompts.

熏蒸消毒前要关紧________和________，密封________，确保圈舍里不能有________和________。

接下来，使用分子悬浮消毒机消毒________。

密封12—24小时后，打开窗________。注意，密封期间一定________进入圈舍。

第21课 Lesson 21

Rù shè zhǔnbèi
入舍准备
Preparation for Entering Animal Pens

复习 Revision

朗读句子。Read the sentences aloud.

1 洗澡间有人。

2 洗澡间没有人。

3 使用高压水枪一定要注意安全。

4 密封期间，一定不能开窗。

热身 Warming Up

看图选词。Look at the pictures and choose the correct words.

A fánghùfú 防护服 protective clothing	B zhuǎnyùnxiāng 转运箱 transfer box
C qín 禽 poultry	D dìmiàn 地面 floor; ground

学习生词 Words and Expressions 21-1

1	入舍	rù shè		enter animal pens
2	什么	shénme	*pron*	what
2	呢	ne	*aux.*	*modal particle*
3	正在	zhèngzài	*adv.*	in the process / course of
4	雏鸡	chújī	*n.*	chick
5	工作	gōngzuò	*n.*	work; job
6	清洁	qīngjié	*adj.*	clean
7	确定	quèdìng	*v.*	determine
8	人员	rényuán	*n.*	staff; personnel

9	分工	fēngōng	*v.*	share the work; divide the jobs
10	防护服	fánghùfú		protective clothing
11	禽	qín	*n.*	poultry
12	转运箱	zhuǎnyùnxiāng		transport box
13	通道	tōngdào	*n.*	entryway; passageway
14	顺畅	shùnchàng	*adj.*	clear; unhindered
15	明亮	míngliàng	*adj.*	well-lit; bright
16	地面	dìmiàn	*n.*	floor; ground
17	干燥	gānzào	*adj.*	dry

词语练习 Words Exercises

1. 将中文词语和对应的拼音及英文连线。Match the Chinese words with corresponding *pinyin* and English words.

1 入舍 •	• qīngjié •	• clean
2 清洁 •	• rù shè •	• determine
3 确定 •	• gānzào •	• dry
4 干燥 •	• quèdìng •	• enter animal pens

2. 词语搭配连线。Match the words.

1 清洁 •	• 时间
2 确定 •	• 分工
3 准备 •	• 圈舍
4 做好 •	• 工具

学习课文 Text 21-2

Rù shè zhǔnbèi
入舍准备

Dàwèi: Nín zài zuò shénme ne?
大卫：您在做什么呢？

Lǐ Shān: Wǒ zhèngzài zuò chújī rù shè zhǔnbèi ne.
李山：我正在做雏鸡入舍准备呢。

Dàwèi: Xūyào zuò nǎxiē gōngzuò?
大卫：需要做哪些工作？

Lǐ Shān: Xiān qīngjié, xiāodú juànshè, ránhòu quèdìng rù shè shíjiān, zuòhǎo rényuán fēngōng. Zhǔnbèi kǒuzhào, shǒutào, fánghùfú, qín zhuǎnyùnxiāng děng gōngjù.
李山：先清洁、消毒圈舍，然后确定入舍时间，做好人员分工。准备口罩、手套、防护服、禽转运箱等工具。

Dàwèi: Xūyào zhùyì shénme ne?
大卫：需要注意什么呢？

Lǐ Shān: Yào quèbǎo rù shè tōngdào shùnchàng, míngliàng, dìmiàn gānzào.
李山：要确保入舍通道顺畅、明亮，地面干燥。

Preparation for Entering Animal Pens

David: What are you doing?

Li Shan: I am preparing for chicks to enter animal pens.

David: What do we need to do?

Li Shan: First, clean and disinfect the pens, then determine the time for chicks to enter the pens and make a good division of labor among the staff. Prepare necessary tools such as masks, gloves, protective clothing, and poultry transport boxes.

David: What should we pay attention to?

Li Shan: Ensure that the entryway to the pens is clear and well-lit, and that the ground is dry.

课文练习 Text Exercises

1. 选词填空。Fill in the blanks with the correct words.

A 通道　　B 正在　　C 清洁　　D 禽转运箱

1. 我________做雏鸡入舍准备呢。
2. 先________、消毒圈舍，然后确定入舍时间。
3. 准备口罩、手套、防护服、________等工具。
4. 要确保入舍________顺畅、明亮，地面干燥。

2. 根据课文内容给下列说法排序。Put the statements in the correct order according to the text.

1. 最后准备口罩、手套、防护服、禽转运箱等工具。
2. 需要做哪些工作？
3. 先清洁、消毒圈舍，
4. 然后确定入舍时间，做好人员分工。

____

学习语法 Grammar

语法点 1 Grammar Point 1

进行态：在 / 正 / 正在 + 动词性短语（+ 呢） The progressive aspect of an action: 在 / 正 / 正在 + 动词性短语（+ 呢）

表示动作的进行或状态的持续，强调说话的时候动作正在进行，状态正在持续。

It indicates the ongoing action or the continuation of a state, emphasizing that the action is in progress or the state is being maintained at the time of speaking.

常用结构：主语 + 在 / 正 / 正在 + 动词性短语（+ 呢）

Common structure: subject + 在 / 正 / 正在 + verb phrase（+ 呢）

例句：

1. Wǒ zhèngzài zuò chújī rù shè zhǔnbèi.
   我 正在 做维鸡入舍准备。I am preparing for chicks to enter animal pens.
2. Wǒ zài chuān gōngzuòfú.
   我在 穿 工作服。I am putting on my working clothes.
3. Dàwèi zhèngzài xiāodú suíshēn wùpǐn ne.
   大卫正在消毒随身物品呢。David is disinfecting his belongings.

语法练习 1 Grammar Exercise 1

用“主语 + 在 / 正 / 正在 + 动词性短语（+ 呢）”连接句子。Connect the sentences with “S+ 在 / 正 / 正在 +VP (+ 呢)”.

1. 消毒圈舍　　我

   ____

2. 组装喷洒设备　　大卫

   ____

3 穿工作服　他

____

4 喷洒泡沫清洁剂　我们

____

语法点 2 Grammar Point 2

语气助词：呢　Model particle: 呢

用在陈述句末，表示动作或者情况正在进行，在“S + 在 / 正在 + VP（+ 呢）”中可省略。

It is used at the end of a declarative sentence to indicate an action or a situation is going on. In the structure of “S + 在 / 正 / 正在 + VP (+ 呢)”, “ 呢 ”can be omitted.

常用结构：主语 + 动词性短语 + 呢

Common structure: subject + verb phrase + 呢

例句：
1 Wǒ zhèngzài zuò chújī rù shè zhǔnbèi ne.
我正在做雏鸡入舍准备呢。I am preparing for chicks to enter animal pens.

2 Wǒ chuān gōngzuòfú ne.
我穿工作服呢。I am putting on my working suit.

3 Dàwèi zài xiāodú suíshēn wùpǐn ne.
大卫在消毒随身物品呢。David is disinfecting his belongings.

语法练习 2 Grammar Exercise 2

用“呢”改写句子。Rewrite the sentences with “ 呢 ”.

1 我在消毒圈舍。

____

2 我们在组装喷洒设备。

____

3 大卫在穿防护服。

---

4 李山在喷洒泡沫清洁剂。

汉字书写 Writing Chinese Characters

wèi 未

mò 末

fū 夫

shī 失

职业拓展 Career Insight

Safety Guideline for Animals Entering Animal Pens

Pigs, cattle, sheep, and other animals are social creatures. When one herds animals, the formation of an animal flow can facilitate our management. Pigs, cattle, sheep, and other animals have a wide range of visual areas, so employees should walk behind the animals and allow them to walk naturally. In order to ensure the safe movement of animals, the number of animals entering the pens at one time should not be too large, and can refer to the requirements in the following table.

Animal	Number of animals moved at one time
Pig	Adult sow: 3–5 sows per time; Adult boar: 1 boar per time; weaning pig: 20–30 weaning pigs per time; Gilt: 5–10 gilts per time.
Cattle	Traction method: 1 head per time; Driving method: 10–20 heads per time.
Chicken	Chick: 80–100 chicks per box; Growing chicken: 1.5kg: 9–10 chickens per box; >3kg: 4–5 chickens per box.

小结 Summary

词语 Words

朗读词语。**Read the words aloud.**

雏鸡	工作	清洁	确定	人员
分工	防护服	转运箱	通道	顺畅
明亮	地面	干燥		

语法 Grammar

语言点回顾。Language points review.

语言点	常用结构	例句
进行态：……在 / 正 / 正在 + 动词性短语（+ 呢）	S + 在 / 正 / 正在 + VP（+ 呢）	我正在做雏鸡入舍准备。 我在穿工作服。
语气助词：呢	S + VP + 呢	我正在做雏鸡入舍准备呢。 我穿工作服呢。

课文理解 Text Comprehension

根据提示复述课文。Retell the text according to the prompts.

雏鸡入舍准备需要做的工作：先________、________圈舍，然后确定入舍________，做好人员________。准备________、________、________、禽________等工具。要确保入舍通道________、________，地面________。

第22课 Lesson 22

Chù-qín rù shè 畜禽入舍 Livestock and Poultry Entering Animal Pens

复习 Revision

朗读句子。Read the sentences aloud.

1. 我在穿工作服。
2. 我穿工作服呢。
3. 我正在做雏鸡入舍准备呢。
4. 我在消毒随身物品。

热身 Warming Up

看图选词。Look at the pictures and choose the correct words.

A 翅膀 (chìbǎng) wing	B 挡猪板 (dǎngzhūbǎn) pig-blocking board
C 牵引绳 (qiānyǐnshéng) leading rope	D 赶猪拍 (gǎnzhūpāi) herding paddle

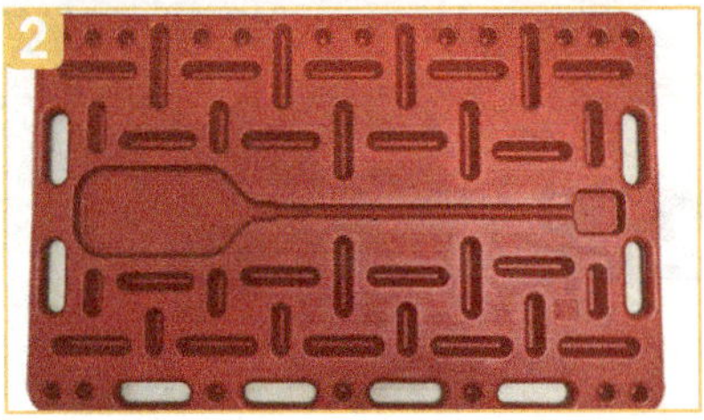

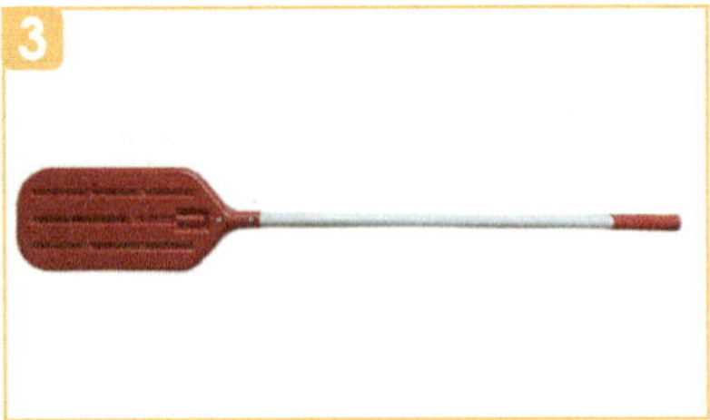

学习生词 Words and Expressions 22-1

1	畜禽	chù-qín		livestock and poultry
2	转	zhuǎn	v.	transfer
3	走	zǒu	v.	walk; go
4	后面	hòumiàn	n.	back
5	挡猪板	dǎngzhūbǎn		pig-blocking board
6	挡	dǎng	v.	keep off
7	身体	shēntǐ	n.	body
8	前面	qiánmiàn	n.	front

9	如果……，就……	rúguǒ..., jiù...		If..., then...
10	动	dòng	*v.*	move
11	赶猪拍	gǎnzhūpāi		herding paddle
12	轻	qīng	*adj.*	gentle
13	拍打	pāidǎ	*v.*	tap
14	牵引绳	qiānyǐnshéng		leadling rope
15	牵	qiān	*v.*	pull; lead along
16	驱赶	qūgǎn	*v.*	herd; drive
17	抬	tái	*v.*	carry; lift; raise
18	到达	dàodá	*v.*	reach; arrive (in / at)
19	抓住	zhuāzhù		grasp
20	翅膀	chìbǎng	*n.*	wing

词语练习 Words Exercises

1. 将中文词语和对应的拼音及英文连线。Match the Chinese words with corresponding *pinyin* and English words.

1 走	qiān	keep off
2 挡	dòng	pull; lead along
3 动	zǒu	walk; go
4 牵	dǎng	move

2. 词语分类。Categorize the words.

A 高压水枪	B 挡猪板	C 水管	D 天平
E 禽转运箱	F 赶猪拍	G 牵引绳	H 高压清洗机

畜禽入舍工具（tools for livestock and poultry entering animal pens）：

学习课文 Text 22-2

Chù-qín rù shè
畜禽入舍

Zhuǎn zhū: Sìyǎngyuán zǒu zài zhū hòumiàn, yòng dǎngzhūbǎn dǎng zài shēntǐ qiánmiàn. Rúguǒ zhū tíngzhǐ bú dòng, jiù yòng gǎnzhūpāi qīngqīng pāida dǎngzhūbǎn.

转猪：饲养员走在猪后面，用挡猪板挡在身体前面。如果猪停止不动，就用赶猪拍轻轻拍打挡猪板。

Zhuǎn niú: Kěyǐ yòng qiānyǐnshéng qiānniú, yě kěyǐ zài niú hòumiàn huǎnmàn qūgǎn.

转牛：可以用牵引绳牵牛，也可以在牛后面缓慢驱赶。

Zhuǎn qín: Liǎng gè rén tái yí ge qín zhuǎnyùnxiāng. Dàodá xīn juànshè hòu, zhuāzhù chìbǎng, bǎ jiāqín fàngdào juànshè li.

转禽：两个人抬一个禽转运箱。到达新圈舍后，抓住翅膀，把家禽放到圈舍里。

Livestock and Poultry Entering Animal Pens

Transferring pigs: The animal keeper walks behind the pigs, using a pig-blocking board in front of the body. If the pigs stop moving, tap the board gently with a herding paddle.

Transferring cows: You can use a leading rope to lead the cows, or you can walk behind them to slowly herd them.

Transferring poultry: Two employees carry a poultry transport box. Once reaching the new pens, grasp the wings of poultry and gently put them inside the pens.

课文练习 Text Exercises

1. 选词填空。Fill in the blanks with the correct words.

A 拍打	B 前面	C 抬	D 驱赶	E 后面

1. 饲养员走在猪________，用挡猪板挡在身体________。
2. 如果猪停止不动，就用赶猪拍轻轻________挡猪板。
3. 可以用牛牵引绳牵牛，也可以在牛后面缓慢________。
4. 两个人________一个禽转运箱。

2. 判断正误。True or false.

1. 如果猪停止不动，就用赶猪拍轻轻拍打猪。

2 不可以用牛牵引绳牵牛。

3 要在牛后面缓慢驱赶。

4 到达新圈舍后，抓住翅膀，把家禽放到圈舍里。

学习语法 Grammar

语法点 1 Grammar Point 1

假设复句：如果……，就……　Suppositive complex sentence: 如果……，就……

用关联词语“如果……，就……”连接两个分句，形成表示假设关系的复句。第一个分句表示假设的前提，第二个分句表示在第一个分句的前提下能够得到的结果。

Use the correlative words “如果……，就……” to connect two clauses and form a complex sentence indicating a hypothetical relationship. The first clause gives a presupposition, and the second clause indicates the result that can be realized from it.

常用结构：如果 + 主语 + 谓语 1，就 + 谓语 2

Common structure: 如果 + subject + predicate1, 就 + predicate2

例句：

1 Rúguǒ zhū tíngzhǐ bú dòng, jiù yòng gǎnzhūpāi qīngqīng pāida dǎngzhūbǎn.
如果猪停止不动，就用赶猪拍轻轻拍打挡猪板。If the pigs stop moving, gently tap the board with a herding paddle.

2 Rúguǒ pēnsǎ jiéshù chāoguò liǎng ge xiǎoshí, jiù kěyǐ yòng shuǐ chōngxǐ xiāodú qūyù.
如果喷洒结束超过两个小时，就可以用水冲洗消毒区域。If the spraying is over for more than two hours, the disinfection area can be rinsed with clean water.

3 Rúguǒ chēngliáng jiéshù, jiù àn “guānjī” jiàn guānjī.
如果称量结束，就按“关机”键关机。If the weighing is finished, press the “ON / OFF” button to power off the balance.

语法练习 1 Grammar Exercise 1

用“如果……，就……”连接句子。Connect the sentences with “如果……，就……”.

1 猪停止不动　　用赶猪拍轻轻拍打挡猪板

____

2 可以用水冲洗消毒区域　　喷洒结束超过两个小时

____

3 称量结束　　按关机键关机

____

4 可以先洒水、浸泡，然后用铁铲清理　　有难清理的污物

____

语法点 2 Grammar Point 2

结果补语：动词 + 住　Complement of result: verb + 住

动词“住”经常用在动词后，做结果补语，表示通过动作使人或事物的位置固定下来，如“记住、接住、站住”。

The verb “住” is often used after a verb to serve as a result complement. It indicates the position of a person or object is fixed by action, for example “记住 (remember)”, “接住 (catch)”, and “站住 (stand still)”.

常用结构：主语 + 动词 + 住 + 宾语

Common structure: subject + verb + 住 + object

例句：

1 Tā zhuāzhù jiāqín de chìbǎng, bǎ jiāqín fàngdào juànshè li.
他抓住家禽的翅膀，把家禽放到圈舍里。He grabbed the poultry by the wings and put it in the pen.

2 Qǐng jìzhù tā de míngzi.
请记住他的名字。Please remember his name.

3 Qǐng názhù gāoyā shuǐqiāng.
请拿住高压水枪。Hold the high-pressure water gun, please.

语法练习 2 Grammar Exercise 2

按照正确的语序连词成句。Make sentences in correct orders with the given words or phrases.

1 ①抓 ②住 ③翅膀 ④家禽的

____

2 ①住 ②牵 ③牛的 ④牵引绳

____

3 ①双手 ②握 ③高压水枪 ④住

____

4 ①用 ②挡住 ③挡猪板 ④身体

____

汉字书写 Writing Chinese Characters

huǒ 火

miè 灭

yán 炎

yàn 焱

文化拓展 Culture Insight

The Bird's Nest

The Bird's Nest Stadium in Beijing, also known as the National Stadium of China, is located in the southern part of the Beijing Olympic Park, serving as the main stadium for the 29th Olympic Games held in 2008. The design inspiration of this stadium comes from the Chinese traditional concept of "nest", with its exterior resembling a bird's nest, symbolizing the nurturing of life and the spreading of hope. This unique design has not only transformed the Bird's Nest Stadium into a landmark in Beijing, but has also gained international acclaim and attention, earning it the distinction of one of the Top Ten Architectural Wonders of the World by *Time* magazine in 2007.

小结 Summary

词语 Words

朗读词语。**Read the words aloud.**

畜禽	后面	挡猪板	前面
赶猪拍	牵引绳	牵	驱赶
抬	到达	抓住	翅膀

语法 Grammar

语言点回顾。Language points review.

语言点	常用结构	例句
假设复句：如果……，就……	如果 + S + P_1，就 + P_2	如果猪停止不动，就用赶猪拍轻轻拍打挡猪板。 如果喷洒结束超过两个小时，就可以用水冲洗消毒区域。
结果补语：动词 + 住	S + V + 住 + O	他抓住家禽的翅膀，把家禽放到圈舍里。 工人握住高压水枪。

课文理解 Text Comprehension

根据提示复述课文。Retell the text according to the prompts.

转猪：饲养员走在猪________，用________挡在身体________。如果猪停止不动，就用赶猪拍________拍打挡猪板。

转牛：可以用牛________牵牛，也可以在牛后面________驱赶。

转禽：两个人抬一个禽________。到达新圈舍后，抓住________，把家禽放到圈舍里。

第23课 Lesson 23

Shǐyòng liàotǒng
使用料桶
Using the Feed Bucket

复习 Revision

朗读句子。Read the sentences aloud.

1 如果猪停止不动，就用赶猪拍轻轻拍打挡猪板。

2 如果喷洒结束超过两个小时，就可以用水冲洗消毒区域。

3 大卫抓住家禽的翅膀，把家禽放到圈舍里。

4 请握住高压水枪。

热身 Warming Up

看图选词。Look at the pictures and choose the correct words.

A 桶身 (tǒngshēn) bucket body	B 饲料 (sìliào) feed
C 料桶 (liàotǒng) feed bucket	D 料盘 (liàopán) feed tray

学习生词 Words and Expressions 23-1

1	料桶	liàotǒng		feed bucket
2	怎么	zěnme	*pron.*	how
3	桶身	tǒngshēn		bucket body
4	插	chā	*v.*	insert
5	料盘	liàopán		feed tray
6	固定	gùdìng	*v.*	fix
7	非常	fēicháng	*adv.*	very; extremely
8	简单	jiǎndān	*adj.*	easy; simple
9	饲料	sìliào	*n.*	feed
10	定期	dìngqī	*adj.*	regular

11	卫生	wèishēng	*n.*	cleanliness; hygiene
12	干净	gānjìng	*adj.*	clean

词语练习 Words Exercises

1. 将中文词语和对应的拼音及英文连线。Match the Chinese words with corresponding *pinyin* and English words.

1 插	gānjìng	simple; easy
2 固定	chā	clean
3 简单	gùdìng	fix
4 干净	jiǎndān	insert

2. 朗读短语。Read the phrases aloud.

1 安装料桶

2 旋转桶身

3 固定料盘

4 定期检查

学习课文 Text 23-2

Shǐyòng liàotǒng
使用料桶

Dàwèi : Zěnme ānzhuāng liàotǒng ne?

大卫 ：怎么安装 料桶呢？

Lǐ Shān : Xiān bǎ tǒngshēn chādào liàopán shang, ránhòu xuánzhuǎn tǒngshēn,
李山：先把桶身插到料盘上，然后旋转 桶身，
gùdìng tǒngshēn hé liàopán.
固定桶身和料盘。

Dàwèi : Zěnme shǐyòng ne?
大卫：怎么使用呢?

Lǐ Shān : Fēicháng jiǎndān. Bǎ liàotǒng fàngdào wéilán li, zài bǎ
李山：非常简单。把料桶放到围栏里，再把
sìliào dàorù liàotǒng. Dìngqī jiǎnchá liàotǒng wèishēng,
饲料倒入料桶。定期检查料桶卫生，
rúguǒ bù gānjìng, jiù xūyào yòng shuǐ qīngxǐ.
如果不干净，就需要用 水清洗。

Using the Feed Bucket

David: How to install the feed bucket?

Li Shan: First, insert the bucket body into the feed tray, and then rotate the bucket to fix it securely to the feed tray.

David: How do I use it?

Li Shan: It is very easy. Place the feed bucket inside the fence and pour the feed into it. Make sure to regularly check if the bucket is clean. If it is dirty, you need to clean it with water.

课文练习 Text Exercises

1. 选词填空。Fill in the blanks with the correct words.

A 放　B 安装　C 固定　D 旋转　E 插　F 倒

1 怎么________料桶呢？

2 把桶身________到料盘上。

3 ________桶身，________桶身和料盘。

4 把料桶________到围栏里，再把饲料________入料桶。

2. 判断正误。True or false.

1 安装料桶的方法：先旋转桶身，然后把桶身插到料盘上。

2 使用料桶的方法：先把饲料倒入料桶，再把料桶放到围栏里。

3 不需要定期检查料桶卫生。

4 如果料桶不干净，就需要用水清洗。

学习语法 Grammar

语法点 1 Grammar Point 1

疑问代词：怎么 interrogative pronoun: 怎么

用在疑问句中，用来对方式、原因等进行提问。使用疑问代词“怎么”提问的时候，句末可以不用语气助词，也可以加语气助词“呢”，但不能加“吗”。

It is used in interrogative sentences to ask about manner, reason, etc. When using the interrogative pronoun “怎么” to ask a question, you can choose not to use a modal particle at the end of the sentence, or you can add the modal particle “呢”, but you should not add “吗” as it is not appropriate.

常用结构：主语 + 怎么 + 动词性短语 / 形容词性短语？

Common structure: subject + 怎么 + verb phrase / adjective phrase?

例句：1 Wǒmen zěnme ānzhuāng liàotǒng ne?
我们怎么安装料桶呢？ How do we install the feed bucket?

2 Zěnme shǐyòng gāoyā shuǐqiāng ne?
怎么使用高压水枪呢？ How do we use the high-pressure water gun?

3 Nǐ zěnme bù gāoxìng?
你怎么不高兴？ Why are you not happy?

语法练习 1 Grammar Exercise 1

按照正确的语序连词成句。Make sentences in correct orders with the given words or phrases.

1 ①组装 ②怎么 ③呢 ④设备 ⑤我们

____

2 ①怎么 ②呢 ③高压水枪 ④使用

____

3 ①料桶 ②使用 ③怎么 ④呢

____

4 ①怎么 ②圈舍 ③消毒

____

语法点 2 Grammar Point 2

程度副词：非常 Adverb of degree: 非常

表示事物性质或心理活动达到很高的程度，比一般的标准高得多。

It indicates that a certain quality of something or a mental activity has reached a high degree, much higher than the normal standard.

常用结构：主语 + 非常 + 形容词

Common structure: subject + 非常 + adjective

例句：
1. Zhège fāngfǎ fēicháng jiǎndān.
这个方法非常简单。This method is very simple.
2. Juànshè fēicháng gānjìng.
圈舍非常干净。The barn is very clean.
3. Wǒmen de yǎngzhíchǎng fēicháng dà.
我们的养殖场非常大。Our livestock and poultry farm is very big.

语法练习 2 Grammar Exercise 2

把“非常”放在句中合适的位置。Put “非常” in the right place of the sentence.

1. 安装料桶____简单。
2. ____难____清理的污物，可以先洒水、浸泡，然后用铁铲清理。
3. 连接泵体跟____高压水枪____难。
4. 生产区到____生活区____远。

汉字书写 Writing Chinese Characters

tǔ 土 土 土

土 土 土 土 土

guī 圭 圭 圭 圭 圭 圭

圭 圭 圭 圭 圭

yáo 垚 垚 垚 垚 垚 垚 垚 垚 垚

垚 垚 垚 垚 垚

chén 尘 尘 尘 尘 尘 尘

尘 尘 尘 尘 尘

职业拓展 Career Insight

Paying Attention to Animal Welfare

Animals enjoy freedom from hunger and thirst, freedom from pain, injury, and disease, freedom from fear and sadness in life, the freedom to express their nature, and the freedom to live in comfort. The freedom to live in comfort involves providing animals with appropriate housing or habitats, ensuring they can obtain comfortable sleep and rest.

小结 Summary

词语 Words

朗读词语。Read the words aloud.

料桶	怎么	桶身	插
料盘	固定	非常	简单
饲料	定期	卫生	干净

语法 Grammar

语言点回顾。Language points review.

语言点	常用结构	例句
疑问代词：怎么	S + 怎么 + VP / AP?	我们怎么安装料桶呢？ 怎么使用高压水枪呢？
程度副词：非常	S + 非常 + Adj	这个方法非常简单。 圈舍非常干净。

课文理解 Text Comprehension

根据提示复述课文。Retell the text according to the prompts.

安装料桶的方法：先旋转________，然后把桶身插到________上。

使用料桶的方法：先把________倒入料桶，再把料桶放到________里。

第24课 Lesson 24

Shǐyòng bǔliàocáo
使用补料槽
Using the Supplemental Feeding Trough

复习 Revision

朗读句子。Read the sentences aloud.

1. 怎么使用高压水枪呢?
2. 我们怎么安装料桶呢?
3. 方法非常简单。
4. 圈舍非常干净。

热身 Warming Up

看图选词。Look at the pictures and choose the correct words.

A 固定杆 (gùdìnggǎn) fixing rod	B 弹簧 (tánhuáng) spring
C 倒钩 (dàogōu) inverted hook	D 螺帽 (luómào) nut

1

2
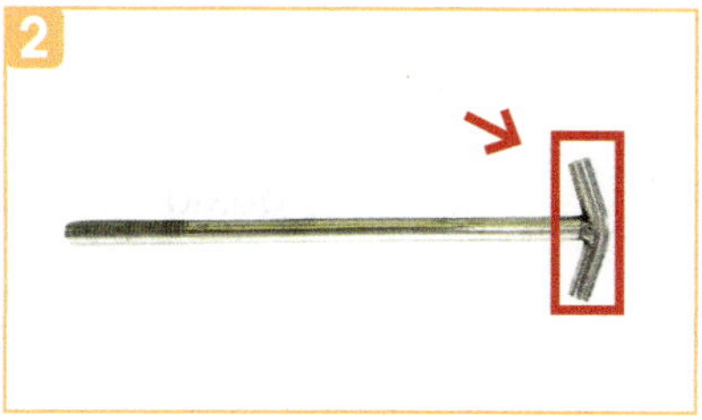

3
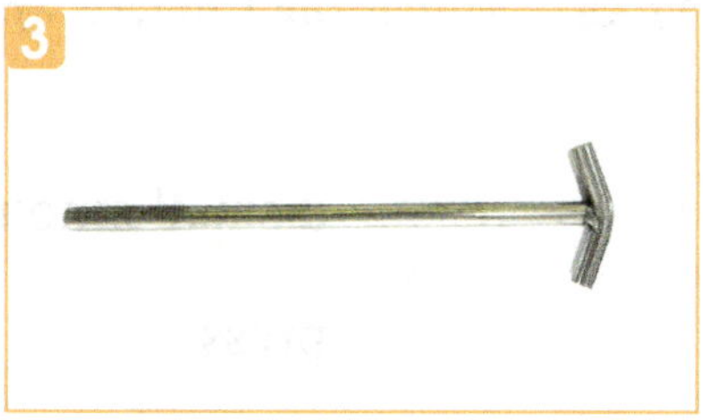

4

学习生词 Words and Expressions 24-1

1	弹簧	tánhuáng	*n.*	spring
2	槽体	cáotǐ		trough body
3	固定杆	gùdìnggǎn		fixing rod
5	按压	ànyā	*v.*	press
4	螺帽	luómào	*n.*	nut
6	底部	dǐbù		bottom
7	倒钩	dàogōu		inverted hook
8	少量	shǎoliàng	*adj.*	a small amount
9	地	de	*aux.*	*structural particle*

10	撒	sǎ	*v.*	scatter; spread
11	取下	qǔxia		take down

词语练习 Words Exercises

1. 将中文词语和对应的拼音及英文连线。Match the Chinese words with corresponding *pinyin* and English words.

1 按压	shǎoliàng	a small amount
2 撒	qǔxià	press
3 取下	ànyā	scatter; spread
4 少量	sǎ	take down

2. 词语搭配连线。Match the words.

1 拧紧	倒钩
2 固定	饲料
3 清洗	圈舍
4 撒	螺帽

学习课文 Text 24-2

Shǐyòng bǔliàocáo
使用补料槽

Dàwèi : Zěnme ānzhuāng bǔliàocáo ne?
大卫：怎么安装补料槽呢？

Lǐ Shān : Xiān bǎ tánhuáng ānzhuāng dào cáotǐ li, zài bǎ gùdìnggǎn ānzhuāng dào tánhuáng li. Zuìhòu ànyā, xuánzhuǎn luómào, bǎ gùdìnggǎn dǐbù de dàogōu gùdìng zài dìbǎn shang.

李山：先把弹簧安装到槽体里，再把固定杆安装到弹簧里。最后按压、旋转螺帽，把固定杆底部的倒钩固定在地板上。

Dàwèi : Ránhòu bǎ sìliào dǎo zài bǔliàocáo li ma?

大卫：然后把饲料倒在补料槽里吗？

Lǐ Shān : Duì, bǎ sìliào jūnyún, shǎoliàng de sǎ zài bǔliàocáo li. Dìngqī jiǎnchá bǔliàocáo de wèishēng, rúguǒ bù gànjìng, jiù xūyào cóng dìbǎn shang qǔxia bǔliàocáo, yòng shuǐ qīngxǐ.

李山：对，把饲料均匀、少量地撒在补料槽里。定期检查补料槽的卫生，如果不干净，就需要从地板上取下补料槽，用水清洗。

Using the Supplemental Feeding Trough

David: How to install the supplemental feeding trough?

Li Shan: First, install the spring into the trough body, and then install the fixing rod into the spring. Finally press and rotate the nut to fix the inverted hook at the bottom of the rod to the floor.

David: Then should I pour the feed into the supplemental feeding trough?

Li Shan: Yes. Scatter the feed evenly in small amounts into the supplemental feeding trough. Regularly check the cleanliness of the trough. If it is dirty, you need to take it down from the floor and clean it with water.

课文练习 Text Exercises

1. 选词填空。Fill in the blanks with the correct words.

A 倒钩　　B 固定杆　　C 补料槽　　D 卫生　　E 槽体

1. 把弹簧安装到________里，再把________安装到弹簧里。
2. 把固定杆底部的________固定在地板上。
3. 把饲料均匀、少量地撒在________里。
4. 定期检查补料槽的________。

2. 根据课文内容给下列说法排序。Put the statements in the correct order according to the text.

1. 再把固定杆安装到弹簧里。
2. 按压、旋转螺帽，把固定杆底部的倒钩固定在地板上。
3. 把饲料均匀、少量地撒在补料槽里。
4. 把弹簧安装到槽体里。

____

学习语法 Grammar

语法点 1 Grammar Point 1

结构助词：地　Structural particle: 地

一般用在状语后、动词或形容词前，是状语的标志。常用于“状语 + 地 + 动词 / 形容词”结构中，“地”前常常是形容词或副词。

It is an adverbial marker usually used after an adverbial modifier and before a verb or an adjective. Often used in "adverbial + 地 + verb / adjective" structure, " 地 " is often preceded by an adjective or adverb.

常用结构：主语 + 形容词 / 副词 + 地 + 动词性短语 / 形容词

Common structure: subject + adjective / adverb + 地 + verb phrase / adjective

例句：1 Dàwèi bǎ sìliào jūnyún de sǎ zài bǔliàocáo li.
大卫把饲料均匀地撒在补料槽里。David scattered the feed evenly in the supplemental feeding trough.

2 Dàwèi qīngqing de pāida gǎnzhūpāi.
大卫轻轻地拍打赶猪拍。David tapped the herding paddle gently.

3 Wǒ dà shēng de dú kèwén.
我大声地读课文。I read the text aloud.

语法练习 1 Grammar Exercise 1

把“地”放在句中合适的位置。Put " 地 " in the right place of the sentence.

1 把饲料少量____洒在____补料槽里。

2 用消毒液均匀____擦拭____随身物品。

3 用赶猪拍轻轻____拍打____挡猪板。

4 把 1000 毫升水缓慢____倒入____量筒。

语法点 2 Grammar Point 2

趋向补语（2）：动词 + 下 Complement of direction (2): verb + 下

趋向补语“下”表示脱离或离开某地方，如“脱下衣服、取下眼镜”。

The directional complement " 下 " indicates separating from or leaving somewhere, for example, " 脱下衣服 (take off clothes)" and " 取下眼镜 (take off glasses)".

例句：

1. Qǐng qǔxia yǎnjìng.
请取下眼镜。Please take off glasses.

2. Qǐng tuōxia gōngzuòfú.
请脱下工作服。Please take off the working clothes.

3. wǒmen xūyào qǔxia bǔliàocáo.
我们需要取下补料槽。We need to take down the feeding trough.

语法练习 2 Grammar Exercise 2

按照正确的语序连词成句。**Make sentences in correct orders with the given words or phrases.**

1. ①请 ②下 ③脱 ④工作服

____

2. ①下 ②他 ③工作鞋 ④脱

____

3. ①眼镜 ②取 ③下 ④大卫

____

4. ①补料槽 ②下 ③我 ④取

____

汉字书写 Writing Chinese Characters

nǐ

你 你 你 你 你 你 你

你	你	你	你	你						

tā 他 他 他 他 他

他	他	他	他	他						

tā 她 她 她 她 她 她

她	她	她	她	她						

tā 它 它 它 它 它

它	它	它	它	它						

文化拓展 Culture Insight

The Culture of Chopsticks

Chopsticks, a tableware invented by the Chinese people, have a history of over 5,000 years. They can be used for picking, poking, clamping, mixing and parting, and are an integral part of traditional Chinese culture. The standard length of chopsticks is seven point six *cuns*, which is about 25 centimeters, symbolizing the seven emotions and six desires of human beings. A pair of chopsticks, consisting of two sticks, represents the harmony of *Yin* and *Yang*, symbolizing that everything in the universe is made up of these two opposing yet complementary forces. The top of chopsticks is square while the bottom is round, signifying the squareness of the heavens and the roundness of the earth.

小结 Summary

词语 Words

朗读词语。Read the words aloud.

弹簧	槽体	固定杆	螺帽
底部	倒钩	撒	取下

语法 Grammar

语言点回顾。Language points review.

语言点	常用结构	例句
结构助词：地	S + Adj / Adv + 地 + VP / Adj	大卫把饲料均匀地撒在补料槽里。 大卫轻轻地拍打赶猪拍。
趋向补语（2）：动词 + 下	V + 下	我们需要取下补料槽。 请脱下工作服。

课文理解 Text Comprehension

根据提示复述课文。Retell the text according to the prompts.

安装补料槽的方法：先把________安装到槽体里，再把________安装到弹簧里。最后按压、旋转________，把固定杆底部的________固定在________上。

使用补料槽的方法：把饲料________、________地撒在补料槽里。定期检查补料槽的________，如果不干净，就需要从地板上________补料槽，用水________。

第25课 Lesson 25

Cāozuò hángchē

操作行车

Operating the Crane

复习 Revision

朗读句子。Read the sentences aloud.

1. 大卫把饲料均匀地撒在补料槽里。
2. 他轻轻地拍打赶猪拍。
3. 我们需要取下补料槽。
4. 他拿出一个口罩。

热身 Warming Up

认读词语。Learn and read the words.

1. 接料口 (jiēliào kǒu) feed receiving port
2. 行车 (hángchē) crane
3. 料仓 (liàocāng) feed bin
4. 加料 (jiāliào) add feed
5. 前进 (qiánjìn) advance
6. 运行 (yùnxíng) (vehicles) move

学习生词 Words and Expressions 25-1

1	行车	hángchē		crane
2	接料口	jiē liào kǒu		feed receiving port
3	加	jiā	*v.*	add
4	加料	jiāliào	*v.*	add feed
5	按钮	ànniǔ	*n.*	button
6	向	xiàng	*prep.*	to; towards
7	料仓	liàocāng		feed bin
8	使	shǐ	*v.*	make; cause; enable
9	前进	qiánjìn	*v.*	advance
10	反向	fǎnxiàng	*v.*	reverse
11	运行	yùnxíng	*v.*	(vehicles) move
12	进行	jìnxíng	*v.*	carry on; conduct
13	第	dì	*prefix*	*marker of ordinal numerals*
14	次	cì	*measure word*	time; occurrence
15	返回	fǎnhuí	*v.*	return

词语练习 Words Exercises

1. 将中文词语和对应的拼音及英文连线。**Match the Chinese words with corresponding *pinyin* and English words.**

1 进行 •	• fǎnhuí •	• return
2 运行 •	• qiánjìn •	• advance
3 返回 •	• jìnxíng •	• carry on; conduct
4 前进 •	• yùnxíng •	• (vehicles) move

2. 词语搭配连线。**Match the words.**

1 按下 •	• 饲料
2 打开 •	• 按钮
3 加 •	• 安全
4 确保 •	• 开关

学习课文 Text 25-2

Cāozuò hángchē
操作行车

Zěnme cāozuò hángchē?
怎么操作行车？

Jiǎnchá hángchē wèizhi, quèbǎo hángchē zài jiē liào kǒu.
1. 检查行车位置，确保行车在接料口。

Ànxia "jiāliào" ànniǔ, xiàng liàocāng li jiāliào.
2. 按下"加料"按钮，向料仓里加料。

Dǎkāi hángchē kāiguān, shǐ hángchē qiánjìn, xiàng liàocáo li jiāliào.
3. 打开行车开关，使行车前进，向料槽里加料。

Dǎkāi hángchē fǎnxiàng yùnxíng kāiguān, jìnxíng dì-èr cì jiāliào. Jiāliào jiéshù hòu, hángchē fǎnhuí dào jiē liào kǒu.
4. 打开行车反向运行开关，进行第二次加料。加料结束后，行车返回到接料口。

Operating the Crane

How to operate the crane?

1. Check the position of the crane, and ensure that it has moved to the feed receiving port.

2. Press the "Feed" button, and add feed to the feed bin.

3. Turn on the crane to move faward and add feed to the feed trough.

4. Turn on the reverse switch of the crane to perform the second round of feeding. Once feeding is complete, the crane returns to the feed receiving port.

课文练习 Text Exercises

1. 选词填空。Fill in the blanks with the correct words.

A 反向　B 料槽　C 行车　D 开关　E 按钮

1 检查________位置，确保行车在接料口。

2 按下“加料”________，向料仓里加料。

3 打开行车________，使行车前进，向________里加料。

4 打开行车________运行开关，进行第二次加料。

2. 根据课文内容给下列说法排序。Put the statements in the correct order according to the text.

1 加料结束后，行车返回到接料口。

2 打开行车反向运行开关，进行第二次加料。

3 检查行车位置，确保行车在接料口。

4 打开行车开关，使行车前进，向料槽里加料。

5 按下“加料”按钮，向料仓里加料。

____

学习语法 Grammar

语法点 1 Grammar Point 1

介词（引出方向、路径）：向　Preposition introducing directions or paths: 向

介词“向”可以引出动作的方向。“向”与表示处所的名词性成分组合，用在动词性成分前，作状语。

The preposition “ 向 ” can introduce the direction of an action. When it is combined with a noun phrase indicating a location and used before a verb phrase, it functions as an adverbial.

常用结构：主语 + 向 + 处所 + 动词性短语

Common structure: subject + 向 + location + verb phrase

Dàwèi xiàng liàocáo li jiāliào.
例句：1 大卫向料槽里加料。David is adding feed to the feeding trough.

Tā xiàng liàotǒng li dàorù sìliào.
2 他向料桶里倒入饲料。He poured feed into the feed bin.

Nǐ xiàng xībian kàn.
3 你向西边看。Look to the west.

语法练习 1 Grammar Exercise 1

把“向”放在句中合适的位置。Put “向” in the right place of the sentence.

1 大卫____喷壶里____装水。

2 他____料桶里____倒入饲料。

3 使____行车____反方向运行。

4 我____量筒里____倒水。

语法点 2 Grammar Point 2

特殊句型：兼语句 Special sentence pattern: pivotal sentence

兼语句是指由兼语短语“动词 1+ 宾语 + 动词 2 / 形容词”充当谓语的句子。“动词 1”的“宾语”同时又是“动词 2 / 形容词”的主语。兼语句一般表示使令意义。

A pivotal sentence refers to a sentence whose predicate is the pivotal phrase “verb1 + object +verb 2 / adjective”. In this structure, the “object” of “verb 1” also serves as the subject of “verb 2”. A pivotal sentences generally conveys a sense of command or causation.

常用结构：主语 + 使 + 宾语 + 动词性短语 / 形容词

Common structure: subject + 使 + object + verb phrase / adjective

例句：1 Tā dǎkāi kāiguān, shǐ hángchē qiánjìn.
他打开开关，使行车前进。He turned on the switch, let the crane to move forward.

2 Wūwù shǐ juànshě hěn nán qīngxǐ.
污物使圈舍很难清洗。The dirt makes it difficult to clean animal pens.

3 Zuò sìyǎngyuán shǐ wǒ kuàilè.
做饲养员使我快乐（happy）。Being an animal keeper makes me happy.

语法练习 2 Grammar Exercise 2

按照正确的语序连词成句。Make sentences in correct orders with the given words or phrases.

1 ①使 ②行车 ③前进 ④他打开开关

____

2 ①我快乐 ②使 ③做饲养员

____

3 ①按“开机”（ON / OFF）键 ②使 ③屏幕 ④显示“0”

____

4 ①圈舍 ②使 ③污渍 ④很难清洗

____

汉字书写 Writing Chinese Characters

hǎo
好 好 好 好 好

nǎi
奶 奶 奶 奶 奶

mā
妈 妈 妈 妈 妈

rú
如 如 如 如 如

职业拓展 Career Insight

Pig Intelligent Feeding System

Pig intelligent feeding system comprises a computer software serving as the control center, multiple feeders acting as the control terminals, and a variety of data-reading sensors (including ear tag recognizers) that feed information to the computer. The control center performs calculations based on the data acquired by the sensors and the scientific feeding algorithms. It then issues instructions to the feeder for precise feeding, ensuring both data and feeding management accuracy for pigs.

小结 Summary

词语 Words

朗读词语。Read the words aloud.

行车	接料口	加料	按钮	向
料仓	使	前进	反向	运行
进行	次	返回		

语法 Grammar

语言点回顾。Language points review.

语言点	常用结构	例句
介词（引出方向、路径）：向	S＋向＋L ＋ VP	大卫在向料槽里加料。 他向料桶里倒入饲料。
兼语句	S＋使＋O＋VP / Adj	他打开开关，使行车前进。 污渍使圈舍很难清洗。

课文理解 Text Comprehension

根据提示复述课文。Retell the text according to the prompts.

怎么操作行车？

1 检查行车________，确保行车在________。

2 按下“加料”按钮，向________里加料。

3 打开行车________，使行车前进，向________里加料。

4 打开行车________运行开关，进行第二次加料。加料结束后，行车________到接料口。

第26课 Lesson 26

Cǎijí shuǐyàng
采集水样
Collecting Water Samples

复习 Revision

朗读句子。Read the sentences aloud.

1. 他向料桶里倒入饲料。
2. 你向东边看。
3. 他打开开关，使行车前进。
4. 污渍使圈舍很难清洗。

热身 Warming Up

看图选词。Look at the pictures and choose the correct words.

A 标签 (biāoqiān) label	B 冰袋 (bīngdài) ice bag
C 保温箱 (bǎowēnxiāng) insulated container	D 水龙头 (shuǐlóngtóu) tap; water faucet

1

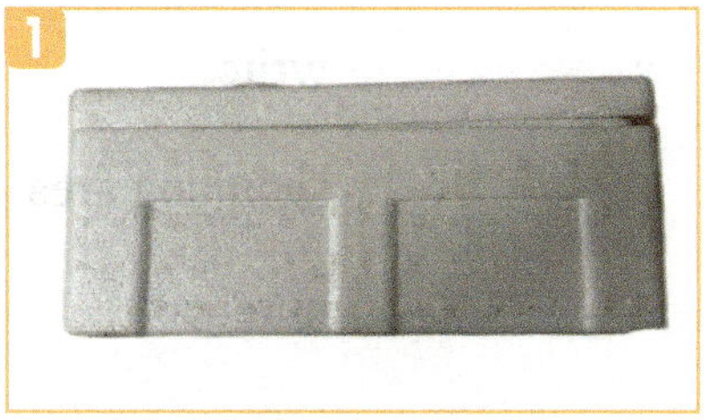

2

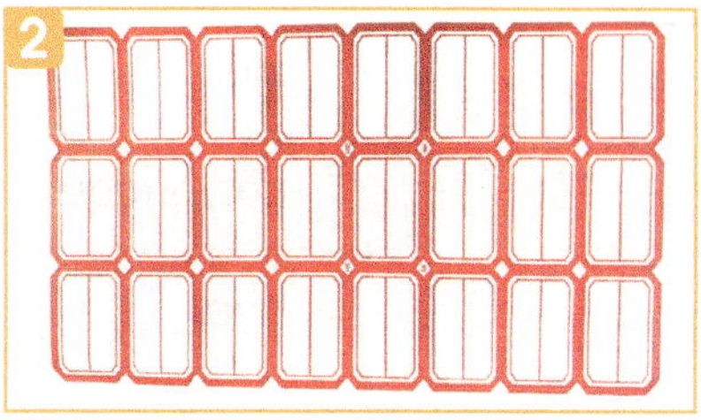

3

4

学习生词 Words and Expressions 26-1

1	采集	cǎijí	*v.*	collect
2	水样	shuǐyàng		water sample
3	水龙头	shuǐlóngtóu	*n.*	tap; water faucet
4	或者	huòzhě	*conj.*	or
5	火焰	huǒyàn	*n.*	flame
6	采样	cǎiyàng	*v.*	take a sample
7	放水	fàng shuǐ		release water
8	无菌管	wújūnguǎn		sterilized sample tube
9	标签	biāoqiān	*n.*	label
10	贴	tiē	*v.*	attach; stick

11	写	xiě	v.	write
12	采样区	cǎiyàngqū		sampling area
13	号	hào	n.	number
14	信息	xìnxī	n.	information
15	保温箱	bǎowēnxiāng		insulated container
16	加入	jiārù	v.	add
17	冰袋	bīngdài	n.	ice bag
18	尽快	jǐnkuài	adv.	as soon as possible
19	送检	sòngjiǎn	v.	send for inspection

词语练习 Words Exercises

1. 将中文词语和对应的拼音及英文连线。Match the Chinese words with corresponding *pinyin* and English words.

1 采集	fàng shuǐ	release water
2 贴	cǎijí	collect
3 放水	sòngjiǎn	send for inspection
4 送检	tiē	attach; stick

2. 词语搭配连线。Match the words.

1 采集	标签
2 贴上	水样
3 放进	时间
4 写下	保温箱

学习课文 Text 26-2

Cǎijí shuǐyàng
采集水样

Zěnme cǎijí shuǐlóngtóu de shuǐyàng?
怎么采集水龙头的水样？

Dì-yī, yòng xiāodúyè huòzhě huǒyàn xiāodú xūyào cǎiyàng de shuǐlóngtou.
第一，用消毒液或者火焰消毒需要采样的水龙头。

Dì-èr, dǎkāi shuǐlóngtóu fàng shuǐ. wǔ fēnzhōng hòu, yòng wǔbǎi háoshēng de wújūnguǎn zhuāngmǎn shuǐyàng, nǐngjǐn gàizi.
第二，打开水龙头放水。5 分钟后，用 500 毫升的无菌管装满水样，拧紧盖子。

Dì-sān, bǎ biāoqiān tiē zài wújūnguǎn shang, xiěxia cǎiyàng shíjiān, cǎiyàngqū, juànshè hào děng xìnxī.
第三，把标签贴在无菌管上，写下采样时间、采样区、圈舍号等信息。

Zuìhòu, bǎ wújūnguǎn fàngjìn bǎowēnxiāng, jiārù bīngdài, jǐnkuài sòngjiǎn.
最后，把无菌管放进保温箱，加入冰袋，尽快送检。

Collecting Water Samples

How to collect water samples from a tap?

First, disinfect the tap that needs to be sampled with disinfectant or by flaming. Second, turn on the tap and release water. Five minutes later, fill a 500-milliliter sterilized sample tube with the water sample and tighten the lid.

Third, attach the label to the sterilized sample tube, write down the sampling time, sampling area, pen number, and other relevant information.

Finally, put the sterilized sample tube into an insulated container, and add ice bags to it. Send the sample for inspection as soon as possible.

课文练习 Text Exercises

1. 选择正确的答案。Choose the correct answers.

1 采样前需要消毒水龙头吗？

A 需要　　B 不需要

2 放水多长时间后开始装水样？

A 2 分钟　　B 10 分钟　　C 5 分钟

3 采样后把什么贴在无菌管上？

A 标签　　B 胶带　　C 纸

4 标签上不需要写什么？

A 采样时间　　B 采样区　　C 采样人

2. 根据课文内容给下列说法排序。**Put the statements in the correct order according to the text.**

1 把无菌管放进保温箱，加入冰袋，尽快送检。

2 把标签贴在无菌管上

3 打开水龙头放水。

4 5 分钟后，用 500 毫升的无菌管装满水样，拧紧盖子。

5 用消毒液消毒需要采样的水龙头。

____

学习语法 Grammar

语法点 1 Grammar Point 1

连词（连接词或者短语）：或者 Conjunction connecting words or phrases: 或者

连词“或者”表示两者或多者中选择其一，用在陈述句中连接词或短语。一般用于陈述句中。

The conjunction “ 或者 ” indicates the choice of one from two or more options, and is used in declarative sentences to connect words or phrases. It is generally used in declarative sentences.

常用结构：A + 或者 / 或 + B

Common structure: A + 或者 / 或 + B

例句：

1 Yòng xiāodúyè huòzhě huǒyàn xiāodú xūyào cǎiyàng de shuǐlóngtóu.
用消毒液或者火焰消毒需要采样的水龙头。Disinfect the tap that needs to be sampled with disinfectant or by flaming.

2 Zuò sìyǎngyuán huòzhě shòuyī dōu xíng.
做饲养员或者兽医都行。Being an animal keeper or a veterinarian is fine.

Yòng zǐwàixiàndēng huòzhě xiāodújì xiāodú suíshēn wùpǐn.
3 用紫外线灯或者消毒剂消毒随身物品。Disinfect personal belongings with UV lamp or disinfectant.

语法练习 1 Grammar Exercise 1

选词填空。**Fill in the blanks with the correct words.**

1 用消毒液________火焰消毒需要采样的水龙头。

2 我叫大卫，________是饲养员。

3 用紫外线灯________消毒液消毒随身物品。

4 围栏需要消毒，墙面________需要消毒。

A 或者

B 也

语法点 2 Grammar Point 2

特殊句型："把"字句（3） Special sentence pattern: the 把 -sentence (3)

指在谓语动词前，由"把"组成的介词性短语作状语的一种句子。由于主语做了某个动作，使"把"后宾语表示的人或事物的状态发生变化。

It is a sentence in which the predicate verb is preceded by an adverbial modifier which is a prepositional phrase formed by " 把 ", indicating that the action performed by the subject has changed the state of the person or thing denoted by the object after " 把 ".

常用结构：主语 + 把 + 宾语 + 动词 + 进 + 处所

Common structure: subject + 把 + object +verb + 进 + location

Tā bǎ wújūnguǎn fàngjìn bǎowēnxiāng.
例句：1 他把无菌管放进保温箱。He put the sterilized sample tube into an insulated container.

Wǒ bǎ yīfu fàngjìn gēngyīshì.
2 我把衣服放进更衣室。I put the clothes into the locker room.

Dàwèi bǎ sìliào dǎojìn liàotǒng.
3 大卫把饲料倒进料桶。David poured the feed into the feed bucket.

语法练习 2 Grammar Exercise 2

按照正确的语序连词成句。Make sentences in correct orders with the given words or phrases.

1 ①把 ②放 ③无菌管 ④进 ⑤保温箱

____

2 ①放 ②把 ③紫外线灯 ④圈舍 ⑤进

____

3 ①泡沫清洁剂 ②把 ③倒 ④喷壶 ⑤进

____

4 ①把 ②饲料 ③料桶 ④进 ⑤放

____

汉字书写 Writing Chinese Characters

zǐ 子 子 子

子	子	子	子	子						

zǎi 仔 仔 仔 仔 仔

仔	仔	仔	仔	仔						

zì 字 字 字 字 字 字

字	字	字	字	字						

xué

学 学 学 学 学 学 学 学

学	学	学	学	学						

文化拓展 Culture Insight

Constant Dropping Water Wears through the Rock

Small drops of water drip down constantly, and they could penetrate even the hardest stones. Although the power seems insignificant, with perseverance and a single-minded purpose, difficult goals can be achieved . This saying is used to describe how perseverance can enable even a small force to achieve great things.

小结 Summary

词语 Words

朗读词语。Read the words aloud.

采集	水样	火焰	采样
无菌管	标签	贴	写
号	信息	保温箱	冰袋

语法 Grammar

语言点回顾。Language points review.

语言点	常用结构	例句
连词（连接词或者短语）：或者	A + 或者 / 或 + B	用消毒液或者火焰消毒需要采样的水龙头。 做饲养员或者兽医都行。
"把"字句（3）：主语 + 把 + 宾语 + 动词 + 进 + 处所	S + 把 + O + V + 进 + L	大卫把无菌管放进保温箱。 我把衣服放进更衣室。

课文理解 Text Comprehension

根据提示复述课文。Retell the text according to the prompts.

怎么采集水龙头的水样？

第一，用消毒液或者________消毒需要采样的________。

第二，打开水龙头放水。5 分钟后，用 500 毫升的________装满水样，拧紧________。

第三，把________贴在无菌管上，写上采样________、采样区、圈舍________等信息。

最后，把无菌管放进________，加入________，尽快________。

第27课 Lesson 27

Qīngjié shuǐxiàn 清洁水线 Cleaning Waterline

复习 Revision

朗读句子。Read the sentences aloud.

1 用消毒液或者火焰消毒需要采样的水龙头。

2 做饲养员或者兽医都行。

3 大卫把无菌管放进保温箱。

4 我把衣服放进更衣室。

热身 Warming Up

看图选词。Look at the pictures and choose the correct words.

A yǐnshuǐqì 饮水器 water dispenser

B jiāyàoqì 加药器 doser

C fámén 阀门 valve

D xiāodúyè 消毒液 disinfectant

1
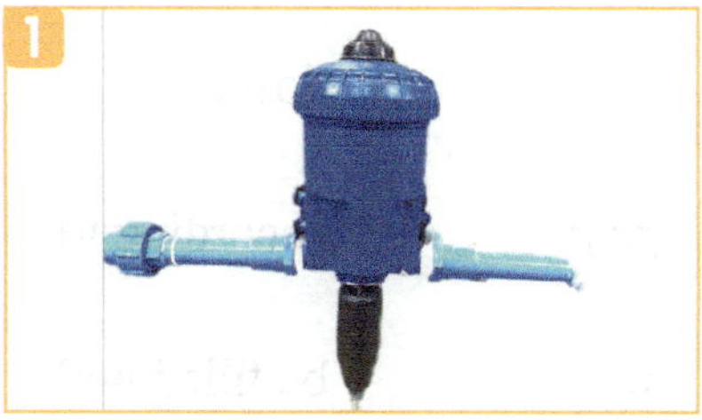

2

3

4

学习生词 Words and Expressions 27-1

1	水线	shuǐxiàn	*n.*	waterline
2	整个	zhěnggè	*adj.*	entire; whole
3	饮水	yǐnshuǐ		drink water
4	系统	xìtǒng	*n.*	system
5	阀门	fámén	*n.*	valve
6	饮水器	yǐnshuǐqì		water dispenser
7	阀杆	fágǎn		valve rod
8	放空	fàngkōng		drain

9	加药器	jiāyàoqì		doser
10	根据	gēnjù	*prep.*	according to
11	充满	chōngmǎn	*v.*	be filled with
12	拆下	chāixia		disassemble
13	才	cái	*adv.*	not until; only when

词语练习 Words Exercises

1. 将中文词语和对应的拼音及英文连线。Match the Chinese words with corresponding *pinyin* and English words.

1 放空	chāixia	according to
2 充满	fàngkōng	be filled with
3 拆下	gēnjù	drain
4 根据	chōngmǎn	disassemble

2. 词语搭配连线。Match the words.

1 关闭	加药器
2 拆下	阀门
3 放空	阀杆
4 按压	消毒液

学习课文 Text 27-2

Qīngjié shuǐxiàn
清洁水线

“Qīngjié shuǐxiàn” shì dìngqī qīngxǐ hé xiāodú chù-qín yǎngzhí de zhěnggè yǐnshuǐ xìtǒng.
“清洁水线”是定期清洗和消毒畜禽养殖的整个饮水系统。

Zěnme qīngjié shuǐxiàn?
怎么清洁水线？

Guānbì jìnshuǐ fámén, ànyā gègè yǐnshuǐqì de fágǎn, fàngkōng shuǐxiàn li de shuǐ.
1. 关闭进水阀门，按压各个饮水器的阀杆，放空水线里的水。

Bǎ jiāyàoqì ānzhuāng zài jìnshuǐ fámén shang. Zài jiāyàoqì jìnshuǐduān fàng xiāodúyè. Gēnjù xūyào, xuánzhuǎn jiāyàoqì xuánniǔ, tiáojié jiāyàoliàng.
2. 把加药器安装在进水阀门上。在加药器进水端放消毒液。根据需要，旋转加药器旋钮，调节加药量。

Dǎkāi liǎng ge jiāyàoqì de fámén, ànyā gègè yǐnshuǐqì de fágǎn, shǐ xiāodúyè chōngmǎn shuǐxiàn.
3. 打开两个加药器的阀门，按压各个饮水器的阀杆，使消毒液充满水线。

Guānbì liǎng ge jiāyàoqì de fámén, chāixia jiāyàoqì. Èrshísì xiǎoshí hòu, cái néng fàngkōng xiāodúyè.
4. 关闭两个加药器的阀门，拆下加药器。24 小时后，才能放空消毒液。

Dǎkāi jìnshuǐ fámén chōngxǐ shuǐxiàn.
5. 打开进水阀门冲洗水线。

Cleaning Waterline

Cleaning waterline involves regularly cleaning and disinfecting the entire drinking water system of livestock and poultry farms.

How to clean a waterline?

1. Turn off the water inlet valve, press the valve rod of each water dispenser to release water, and drain the waterline completely.

2. Install the doser on the water inlet valve. Add disinfectant into the inlet end of the doser. Adjust the dosage by rotating the knob of the doser according to actual needs.

3. Turn on both valves of the doser, and press the valve rod of each water dispenser to ensure that the disinfectant fills the entire waterline.

4. Allow the disinfectant to remain in the waterline for 24 hours. After this period, turn off both valves of the doser, disassemble the doser, and drain the disinfectant from the waterline.

5. Turn on the water inlet valve and rinse the waterline thoroughly.

课文练习 Text Exercises

1. 选择正确的答案。Choose the correct answers.

1 放空水线里的水前，需要关闭什么？

A 进水阀门　　B 出水阀门　　C 总阀门

2 怎么调节加药器的加药量？

A 打开进水阀门　　B 旋转加药器旋钮　　C 打开出水阀门

3 需要打开几个加药器阀门才能使消毒液充满水线？

A 一个　　B 两个　　C 三个

4 多长时间后，才能放空水线里的消毒液？

A 十个小时　　B 二十个小时　　C 二十四个小时

2. 根据课文内容给下列说法排序。Put the statements in the correct order according to the text.

1 打开两个加药器阀门，按压各个饮水器的阀杆，使消毒液充满水线。

2 关闭进水阀门，按压各个饮水器的阀杆，放空水线里的水。

3 安装加药器，放消毒液。根据需要，旋转加药器旋钮，调节加药量。

4 关闭两个加药器阀门，拆下加药器。24 小时后放空消毒液。

5 打开进水阀门冲洗水线。

学习语法 Grammar

语法点 1 Grammar Point 1

介词：根据　Preposition: 根据

介词“根据”后面加名词性成分组成介词结构，表示以某种事物为基础和前提。一般用在句首。

The preposition “根据” is followed by a noun phrase to form a prepositional phrase, indicating that something is based on or preceded by a certain object. It is generally used at the beginning of a sentence.

常用结构：根据 + 名词性短语，……

Common structure: 根据 + noun phrase，……

例句：

1. Gēnjù xūyào, xuánzhuǎn jiāyàoqì xuánniǔ, tiáojié jiāyàoliàng.
根据需要，旋转加药器旋钮，调节加药量。Adjust the dosage by rotating the knob of the doser according to actual needs.

2. Gēnjù bǐlì yāoqiú, xuánzhuǎn pēnhú xuánniǔ.
根据比例要求，旋转喷壶旋钮。Rotate the spray bottle knob according to the proportion requirements.

3. Gēnjù fánghù yāoqiú, chuānhǎo yǔyī, yǔkù, jiāoxié.
根据防护要求，穿好雨衣、雨裤、胶鞋。Wear raincoats, rain pants, and rubber shoes according to the protective requirements.

语法练习 1 Grammar Exercise 1

把“根据”放在句中合适的位置。Put “根据” in the right place of the sentence.

1. ____需要，____旋转加药器旋钮，调节加药量。
2. ____参数要求，____按“+”“－”键设置喷洒时间。

3 ____消毒液的比例和总量，____计算水和消毒药品的用量。

4 ____入舍时间，____进行人员分工。

语法点 2 Grammar Point 2

语气副词：才 Adverb of mood: 才

语气副词“才”用在动词前面，表示说话人认为事情发生得比预想得晚，也可表达数量少、程度低等，具有较强的主观性。

The adverb of mood “才” is used before a verb to indicate that the speaker believes the event occurred later than expected, or to express a small quantity or low degree, with a strong subjective nature.

常用结构：主语 + 数量短语 / 名词性短语 + 才 + 动词性短语

Common structure: subject + numeral phrase / noun phrase + 才 + verb phrase

例句：

1 Èrshísì xiǎoshí hòu, cái néng fàngkōng xiāodúyè.
24 小时后，才能放空消毒液。The disinfectant cannot be drained until 24 hours later.

2 Bā diǎn kāishǐ, Dàwèi jiǔ diǎn cái lái.
8 点开始，大卫 9 点才来。It started at 8 o’clock, but David only arrived at 9 o’clock.

3 Juànshè li cái yǒu wǔ zhī yáng.
圈舍里才有 5 只羊。There are only five sheep in the animal pen.

语法练习 2 Grammar Exercise 2

按照正确的语序连词成句。Make sentences in correct orders with the given words or phrases.

1 ①才 ②两个小时后 ③能用水冲洗消毒区域

____

2 ①是合适的温度 ②才 ③ 20℃

____

3 ①他 ②到办公楼 ③才

____

4 ① 24 小时候后 ②可以放空消毒液 ③才

____

汉字书写 Writing Chinese Characters

kě 可 可 可 可 可

可	可	可	可	可						

hé 何 何 何 何 何 何 何

何	何	何	何	何						

hé 河 河 河 河 河 河 河 河

河	河	河	河	河						

hē 呵 呵 呵 呵 呵 呵 呵 呵

呵	呵	呵	呵	呵						

职业拓展 Career Insight

Paying Attention to Water Quality and Safety

The quality of drinking water for livestock and poultry generally concerns hardness, salt content, and bacterial count in water. The hardness of water mainly refers to the concentration of calcium ions, the salt content in water mainly refers to the concentration of chloride ions, and the primary bacterial types include Escherichia coli, Salmonella, etc.

小结 Summary

词语 Words

朗读词语。Read the words aloud.

水线	阀门	饮水器	阀杆
放空	加药器	进水端	根据
充满	拆下	才	

语法 Grammar

语言点回顾。Language points review.

语言点	常用结构	例句
介词：根据	根据 + NP，……	根据需要，旋转加药器旋钮，调节加药量。 根据泡沫清洁剂和水的比例要求，旋转喷壶旋钮。
语气副词：才	S + NumP / NP + 才 + VP	24 小时后，才能放空消毒液。 8 点开始，大卫 9 点才来。

课文理解 Text Comprehension

根据提示复述课文。Retell the text according to the prompts.

“清洁水线”是定期清洗和消毒畜禽养殖的整个饮水系统。

怎么清洁水线？

1 关闭________阀门，按压各个________的________，放空水线里的________。

2 把________安装在进水阀门上。在加药器进水端放________。根据需要，旋转加药器________，调节加药量。

3 打开________加药器的阀门，按压各个饮水器的阀杆，使消毒液________水线。

4 关闭两个加药器的________，拆下加药器。24 小时后，才能________消毒液。

5 打开进水阀门________水线。

第28课
Lesson 28

Tiáojié yǐnshuǐliàng
调节饮水量
Regulating Water Intake

复习 Revision

朗读句子。**Read the sentences aloud.**

1. 根据需要，旋转加药器旋钮。
2. 根据泡沫清洁剂和水的比例要求，旋转喷壶旋钮。
3. 24 小时后，才能放空消毒液。
4. 圈舍里才有 5 只羊。

热身 Warming Up

看图选词。**Look at the pictures and choose the correct words.**

A 容器 (róngqì) container; vessel	B 矿泉水瓶 (kuàngquánshuǐpíng) mineral water bottle
C 计时器 (jìshíqì) timer	

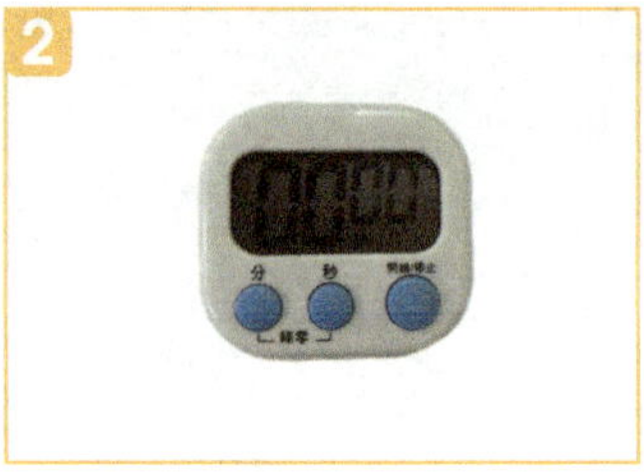

学习生词 Words and Expressions 28-1

1	饮水量	yǐnshuǐliàng		water intake
2	容器	róngqì	*n.*	container; vessel
3	矿泉水瓶	kuàngquánshuǐpíng		mineral water bottle
4	计时	jìshí	*v.*	reckon by time
5	计时器	jìshíqì		timer
6	一边……，一边……	yībiān..., yībiān...		at the same time; while
7	接	jiē	*v.*	take
8	判断	pànduàn	*v.*	judge
9	是否	shìfǒu	*adv.*	whether or not
10	标准	biāozhǔn	*n.*	standard
11	要是……，就……	yàoshi..., jiù...		If..., (then)...
12	够	gòu	*v.*	be enough
13	开大	kāidà		turn up

14	相反	xiāngfǎn	*conj.*	on the contrary
15	关小	guānxiǎo		turn down

词语练习 Words Exercises

1. 将中文词语和对应的拼音及英文连线。Match the Chinese words with corresponding *pinyin* and English words.

1 容器	biāozhǔn	timer
2 计时器	róngqì	container; vessel
3 标准	xiāngfǎn	on the contrary
4 相反	jìshíqì	standard

2. 选词填空。Fill in the blanks with the correct words.

A 计时　　B 接　　C 关小　　D 调节

1 ____水　　2 开始____　　3 ____阀门　　4 ____饮水量

学习课文 Text 28-2

Tiáojié yǐnshuǐliàng
调节饮水量

Zhǔnbèi wǔbǎi háoshēng de róngqì (rú kuàngquánshuǐpíng) hé
准备500毫升的容器（如矿泉水瓶）和

jìshíqì.　Ànyā yǐnshuǐqì de fágǎn,　yìbiān yòng róngqì jiē shuǐ,
计时器。按压饮水器的阀杆，一边用容器接水，
yìbiān kāishǐ jìshí.　yì fēnzhōng hòu,　tíngzhǐ jiē shuǐ.
一边开始计时。一分钟后，停止接水。

Gēnjù róngqì li de shuǐliàng,　pànduàn chūshuǐliàng shìfǒu dádào
根据容器里的水量，判断出水量是否达到
biāozhǔn.　yàoshi chūshuǐliàng bú gòu,　jiù xūyào kāidà fámén.
标准。要是出水量不够，就需要开大阀门。
xiāngfǎn,　jiù xūyào guānxiǎo fámén.
相反，就需要关小阀门。

Regulating Water Intake

Prepare a 500-milliliter container (e.g., mineral water bottle) and a timer. Press the valve rod of the water dispenser and start the timer while filling the container with water. After one minute, stop filling the water.

According to the amount of water in the container, you can judge whether the amount of outflow within one minute meets the standard. If the outflow is not enough, you need to increase the water flow by turning up the valve. On the contrary, you need to turn down the water flow by turning down the valve.

课文练习 Text Exercises

1. 选择正确的答案。Choose the correct answers.

1 调节饮水量时，需要准备什么？

A 500 毫升的容器和计时器　　B 500 毫升的容器　　C 计时器

2 开始计时后，多长时间停止接水？

A 三分钟　　B 五分钟　　C 一分钟

3 要是出水量不够需要怎么做？

A 开大阀门　　B 关小阀门　　C 关闭阀门

2. 根据课文内容给下列说法排序。Put the statements in the correct order according to the text.

1 根据容器里的水量，判断出水量是否达到标准。

2 一分钟后，停止接水。

3 按压饮水器的阀杆，一边用容器接水，一边开始计时。

4 准备 500 毫升的容器（如矿泉水瓶）和计时器。

____

学习语法 Grammar

语法点 1 Grammar Point 1

并列复句：一边……，一边…… Coordinate complex sentence: 一边……，一边……

由“一边……，一边……”连续两个分句，描述两个动作同时进行。

Two clauses connected by "一边……，一边……" describe two actions going on simultaneously.

常用结构：主语 + 一边 + 动词性短语 1，一边 + 动词性短语 2

Common structure: subject + 一边 + verb phrase 1,+ 一边 + verb phrase 2

例句：1 Wǒ yìbiān yòng róngqì jiē shuǐ, yìbiān kāishǐ jìshí.
我一边用容器接水，一边开始计时。I started timing while catching water with a container.

2 Wǒmen yìbiān yòng dǎngzhūbǎn dǎng zài shēntǐ qiánmiàn, yìbiān yòng gǎnzhūpāi qīngqīng pāida dǎngzhūbǎn.
我们一边用挡猪板挡在身体前面，一边用赶猪拍轻轻拍打挡猪板。We use a pig-blocking board in front of our bodies, and gently tap the board with a herding paddle.

3 Tā yìbiān tīng lùyīn yìbiān liànxí shuō Zhōngwén.
他一边听录音一边练习说中文。He practices speaking Chinese while listening to the tape.

语法练习 1 Grammar Exercise 1

用"一边……，一边……"连接句子。Connect the sentences with "一边……，一边……".

1 我　打开水龙头放水　注意时间

____

2 他　按高压水枪扳机　控制冲洗方向

____

3 大卫　看行车　打开开关

____

4 他　听录音　练习说中文

____

语法点 2 Grammar Point 2

假设复句：要是……，就…… Suppositive complex sentence: 要是……，就……

前一分句提出假设，后一分句表示假设实现后所产生的结果。

The first clause puts forward a supposition, and the second clause indicates the result that will come about when this supposition is realized.

常用结构：要是 + 主语 + 谓语 1，就 + 谓语 2

Common structure: 要是 + subject + predicate 1, 就 + predicate 2

例句：

1. Yàoshi chūshuǐliàng bú gòu, jiù xūyào kāidà fámén.
要是出水量不够，就需要开大阀门。If the outflow is not enough, you need to increase the water flow by turning up the valve.

2. Yàoshi zhū tíngzhǐ búdòng, jiù yòng gǎnzhūpāi qīngqīng pāida dǎngzhūbǎn.
要是猪停止不动，就用赶猪拍轻轻拍打挡猪板。If the pigs stop moving, gently tap the board with a herding paddle.

3. Yàoshi bù xiāodú, jiù bù néng jìn juànshè.
要是不消毒，就不能进圈舍。If it is not disinfected, you cannot enter animal pens.

语法练习 2 Grammar Exercise 2

按照正确的语序连词成句。Make sentences in correct orders with the given words or phrases.

1. ①要是 ②出水量不够 ③需要开大闸门 ④就

____

2. ①喷洒泡沫清洁剂 ②要是 ③就 ④要穿雨衣

____

3. ①就 ②污物很难清理 ③要是 ④先洒水、浸泡

____

4 ①需要关小阀门 ②要是 ③出水量很大 ④就

____

汉字书写 Writing Chinese Characters

rén 仁

仁	仁	仁	仁	仁						

sā 仨

仨	仨	仨	仨	仨						

xiū 休

休	休	休	休	休						

tǐ 体

体	体	体	体	体						

文化拓展 Culture Insight

When Drinking Water, Remember Its Source

"When drinking water, one should not forget its source" means to remember where the water comes from when you drink it. It refers to people who live in a foreign country and will eventually return to their hometown. It is a metaphor suggesting that things have a certain destination, emphasizing that one should not forget his root.

小结 Summary

词语 Words

朗读词语。Read the words aloud.

饮水量	容器	矿泉水瓶	计时
计时器	一边……，一边……		接
判断	是否	标准	够
要是……，就……		相反	关小

语法 Grammar

语言点回顾。Language points review.

语言点	常用结构	例句
并列复句：一边……，一边……	S + 一边 + VP_1，一边 + VP_2	我一边用容器接水，一边开始计时。 我们一边用挡猪板挡在身体前面，一边用赶猪拍轻轻拍打挡猪板。
要是……，就…… If..., (then)...	要是 + S + P_1，就 + P_2	要是出水量不够，就需要开大阀门。 要是猪停止不动，就用赶猪拍轻轻拍打挡猪板。

课文理解 Text Comprehension

根据提示复述课文。Retell the text according to the prompts.

准备500毫升的________（如矿泉水瓶）和________。按压________的阀杆，一边用容器________，一边开始________。一分钟后，停止接水。

根据容器里的________，判断出水量是否达到________。要是出水量不够，就需要________阀门。相反，就需要关小阀门。

第29课 Lesson 29

Ānzhuāng bǎowēndēng
安装保温灯
Installing Heat Lamps

复习 Revision

朗读句子。Read the sentences aloud.

1. 我一边用容器接水，一边开始计时。
2. 大卫一边听录音，一边练习说中文。
3. 要是出水量不够，就需要开大阀门。
4. 要是猪停止不动，就用赶猪拍轻轻拍打挡猪板。

热身 Warming Up

看图选词。Look at the pictures and choose the correct words.

A 灯罩 (dēngzhào) lamp shade	B 灯头 (dēngtóu) lamp cap
C 灯泡 (dēngpào) lamp bulb	D 铁丝网罩 (tiěsī wǎngzhào) wire mesh cover

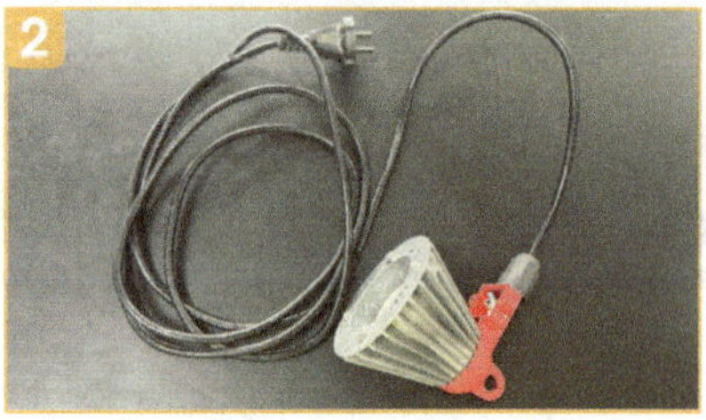

学习生词 Words and Expressions 29-1

1	灯头	dēngtóu	*n.*	lamp cap
2	灯罩	dēngzhào	*n.*	lamp shade
3	红外线	hóngwàixiàn	*n.*	infrared; infrared ray
4	灯泡	dēngpào	*n.*	lamp bulb
5	盖	gài	*v.*	cover
6	铁丝网罩	tiěsī wǎngzhào		wire mesh cover
7	吊链	diàoliàn		hanging chain
8	挂	guà	*v.*	hang

9	上方	shàngfāng		high place; higher position
10	离	lí	*prep.*	be (away) from
11	大约	dàyuē	*adv.*	about; around
12	厘米	límǐ	*measure word*	centimeter
13	档位	dàngwèi	*n.*	level; grade

词语练习 Words Exercises

1. 将中文词语和对应的拼音及英文连线。Match the Chinese words with corresponding *pinyin* and English words.

1 盖	guà	around; about
2 挂	gài	level; grade
3 大约	dàngwèi	cover
4 档位	dàyuē	hang

2. 选词填空。Fill in the blanks with the correct words.

A 挂在　B 调节　C 离　D 打开　E 大约　F 盖好　G 组装

1 ________ 灯头和灯罩，把红外线灯泡安装在灯头上。

2 ________ 铁丝网罩，把吊链 ________ 围栏上方。

3 确保灯罩 ________ 地面 ________ 45 厘米。

4 ________ 开关，________ 档位。

学习课文 Text 29-2

Ānzhuāng bǎowēndēng
安装 保温灯

Xiān zǔzhuāng dēngtóu hé dēngzhào, ránhòu bǎ hóngwàixiàn dēngpào
先组装灯头和灯罩，然后把红外线灯泡

ānzhuāng zài dēngtóu shang, gàihǎo tiěsī wǎngzhào. Jiēxiàlai, bǎ diàoliàn
安装在灯头上，盖好铁丝网罩。接下来，把吊链

guà zài wéilán shàngfāng, quèbǎo dēngzhào lí dìmiàn dàyuē sìshíwǔ límǐ.
挂在围栏上方，确保灯罩离地面大约 45 厘米。

Zuìhòu liánjiē diànyuán, dǎkāi kāiguān, tiáojié dàngwèi.
最后连接电源，打开开关，调节档位。

Installing Heat Lamps

First assemble the lamp cap and lamp shade, then install the infrared light bulb on the lamp cap, tightly fix the wire mesh cover. Next, hang the hanging chain over the fence, ensuring that the lamp shade is about 45 centimeters from the ground. Finally, connect the power source, turn on the switch, and adjust the heat level.

课文练习 Text Exercises

1. 选词填空。Fill in the blanks with the correct words.

A 调节　　B 连接　　C 挂　　D 安装　　E 离

1 把红外线灯泡________在灯头上。

2 把吊链________在围栏上方。

3 确保灯罩________地面大约 45 厘米。

4 最后________电源，打开开关，________档位。

2. 按照正确的语序连词成句。Make sentences in correct orders with the given words or phrases.

1 把红外线灯泡安装在灯头上

2 连接电源，打开开关，调节档位

3 组装灯头和灯罩

4 盖好铁丝网罩

5 把吊链挂在围栏上方

____

学习语法 Grammar

语法点 1 Grammar Point 1

介词（引出对象）：离　Preposition introducing object: 离

用于引出目标。"离"一般与名词性成分组合；但表示时间时，也可与动词性成分组合使用。

It introduces the goal. "离" is generally combined with nominal components; however, when expressing time, it can also be used in combination with verbal components.

常用结构：A + 离 + B + 动词性短语 / 形容词性短语

Common structure: A + 离 + B + verb phrase / adjective phrase

例句：

1. Dēngzhào lí dìmiàn dàyuē sìshíwǔ límǐ.
灯罩离地面大约45厘米。The lampshade is about 45 centimeters from the ground.

2. Liàocáo lí wéilán hěn jìn.
料槽离围栏很近。The feed trough is very close to the fence.

3. Xiànzài lí xiāodú jiéshù hái yǒu yí ge xiǎoshí.
现在离消毒结束还有1个小时。There is still one hour left before the disinfection ends.

语法练习1 Grammar Exercise 1

根据提示练习说句子。**Practice speaking sentences according to the prompts.**

1. 办公楼 ←1000米→ 食堂

____

2. 
↕ 70cm
地面

____

3. 篮球场 ←500米→ 宿舍

____

4. 圈舍 ←50米→ 

____

语法点 2 Grammar Point 2

概数表示法：大约 Expression of approximate number: 大约

“大约”用于数词前边，表示跟数词接近的大概数目。

“ 大约 ” is used before a numeral to indicate a number close to the numeral.

常用结构：大约（+ 动词）+ 数量短语（+ 名词）

Common structure: 大约 (+ verb) + numeral phrase (+ noun)

例句：

1. Dēngzhào lí dìmiàn dàyuē sìshíwǔ límǐ.
   灯罩离地面大约 45 厘米。The lampshade is about 45 centimeters from the ground.
2. Yǎngzhíchǎng dàyuē yǒu èrbǎi tóu niú.
   养殖场大约有 200 头牛。The farm has approximately 200 cows.
3. Wǒmen gōngsī dàyuē yǒu sānshí ge rén.
   我们公司大约有 30 个人。Our company has about 30 people.

语法练习 2 Grammar Exercise 2

按照正确的语序连词成句。Make sentences in correct orders with the given words or phrases.

1. ①大约 ②45 厘米 ③灯罩 ④离地面

   ____
2. ①消毒 ②圈舍 ③大约 ④2 个小时

   ____
3. ①冲洗 ②15 分钟 ③大约

   ____
4. ①20 头 ②大约 ③牛

   ____

汉字书写 Writing Chinese Characters

jiāng 江 江 江 江 江 江

江 江 江 江 江

hé 河 河 河 河 河 河 河 河

河 河 河 河 河

hú 湖 湖 湖 湖 湖 湖 湖 湖 湖 湖 湖 湖

湖 湖 湖 湖 湖

hǎi 海 海 海 海 海 海 海 海 海 海

海 海 海 海 海

职业拓展 Career Insight

Adjusting the Lighting Parameters Timely

In the production of livestock and poultry, attention should be paid not only to the time and intensity of light, but also to the uniformity and stability of it. During the production process, the light intensity may diminish due to the aging of the bulbs or tubes. Based on the measurement results, adjustments should be made using a continuous adjustable transformer.

小结 Summary

词语 Words

朗读词语。Read the words aloud.

灯头	灯罩	红外线	灯泡	盖
铁丝网罩		吊链	挂	上方
离	大约	厘米	档位	

语法 Grammar

语言点回顾。Language points review.

语言点	常用结构	例句
介词（引出对象）：离	A + 离 + B + VP / AP	灯罩离地面大约 45 厘米。 料槽离围栏很近。
概数表示法：大约	大约 (+ V) + NumP (+ N)	灯罩离地面大约 45 厘米。 养殖场大约有 200 头牛。

课文理解 Text Comprehension

根据提示复述课文。Retell the text according to the prompts.

先组装灯头和________，然后把红外线灯泡安装在________上，盖好________。接下来，把________挂在围栏上方，确保灯罩离地面大约________厘米。最后连接电源，打开________，调节________。

第30课 Lesson 30

Ānzhuāng bǎowēnsǎn
安装保温伞
Installing Brooders

复习 Revision

朗读句子。Read the sentences aloud.

1. 灯罩离地面大约 45 厘米。
2. 现在离消毒结束还有 1 个小时。
3. 养殖场大约有 200 头牛。
4. 我们公司大约有 30 个人。

热身 Warming Up

认读词语。Learn and read the words.

1. bǎowēnsǎn 保温伞 brooder
2. tiětiáo 铁条 iron bar
3. gāodù 高度 height
4. jùlí 距离 be part / away from
5. píngtái 平台 platform
6. lèixíng 类型 type

学习生词 Words and Expressions 30-1

1	保温伞	bǎowēnsǎn		brooder
2	首先	shǒuxiān	*adv.*	first
3	根	gēn	*measure word*	*(for long / thin objects)*
4	铁条	tiětiáo		iron bar
5	悬挂	xuánguà	*v.*	hang
6	调整	tiáozhěng	*v.*	adjust
7	平行	píngxíng	*v.*	be parallel to
8	高度	gāodù	*n.*	height
9	比	bǐ	*prep.*	than
10	低	dī	*adj.*	low
11	距离	jùlí	*v.*	be part / away from
12	平台	píngtái	*n.*	platform
13	类型	lèixíng	*n.*	type
15	加热管	jiārèguǎn		heat tube

词语练习 Words Exercises

1. 将中文词语和对应的拼音及英文连线。Match the Chinese words with corresponding *pinyin* and English words.

1 悬挂	lèixíng	type
2 平行	gāodù	hang
3 高度	píngxíng	be parallel to
4 类型	xuánguà	height

2. 选词填空。Fill in the blanks with the correct words.

A 平行　　B 悬挂　　C 调整　　D 安装

1. ________保温伞
2. 与地面________
3. ________高度
4. ________加热管

学习课文 Text 30-2

ānzhuāng bǎowēnsǎn
安装 保温伞

Shǒuxiān bǎ bǎowēnsǎn yòng yì gēn tiětiáo xuánguà zài wéilán shàngfāng, ránhòu tiáozhěng bǎowēnsǎn, shǐ bǎowēnsǎn hé dìmiàn píngxíng. Bǎowēnsǎn de xuánguà gāodù bǐ bǎowēndēng dī, jùlí yǎngzhí píngtái dàyuē èrshíwǔ dào sānshí límǐ. Gēnjù bǎowēnsǎn de lèixíng, ānzhuāng hóngwàixiàn dēngpào huòzhě jiārèguǎn. Zuìhòu liánjiē diànyuán, dǎkāi kāiguān, tiáojié dàngwèi.

首先把保温伞用一根铁条悬挂在围栏上方，然后调整保温伞，使保温伞和地面平行。保温伞的悬挂高度比保温灯低，距离养殖平台大约 25—30 厘米。根据保温伞的类型，安装红外线灯泡或者加热管。最后连接电源，打开开关，调节档位。

Installing Brooders

First, hang a brooder using an iron bar above the fence, and then adjust the brooder to ensure it is parallel to the ground. The brooder should be hung at a height lower than that of the heat lamp, about 25 to 30 centimeters above the breeding platform. Depending on the type of brooder, install infrared light bulb or a heat tube. Finally, connect the power source, turn on the switch, and adjust the heat level.

课文练习 Text Exercises

1. 选择正确的答案。Choose the correct answers.

1 保温伞要和地面平行吗？____

A 是的　　B 不是

2 保温伞的悬挂高度比保温灯低吗？____

A 是的　　B 不是

3 保温伞距离养殖平台大约____厘米。

A 15—20　　B 20—25　　C 25—30

4 根据保温伞类型，安装____或者____。

A 红外线灯泡　　B 加热管

2. 根据课文内容给下列说法排序。Put the statements in the correct order according to the text.

1 把保温伞用一根铁条挂在围栏上方。

2 连接电源，打开开关，调节档位。

3 根据保温伞类型，安装红外线灯泡或发热管。

4 调整保温伞，使保温伞和地面平行。

学习语法 Grammar

语法点 1 Grammar Point 1

承接复句：首先……，然后……　Successive complex sentence: 首先……，然后……

用于列举事项，表示一件事情之后，接着发生另一件事情。

It is used to enumerate items, indicating that one thing happened first and then something else.

常用结构：主语＋首先＋谓语 1，然后＋谓语 2

Common structure: subject + 首先 + predicate 1, 然后 + predicate 2

例句：

1 Shǒuxiān bǎ bǎowēnsǎn yòng yì gēn tiětiáo xuánguà zài wéilán shàngfāng, ránhòu tiáozhěng bǎowēnsǎn, shǐ bǎowēnsǎn hé dìmiàn píngxíng.
首先把保温伞用一根铁条悬挂在围栏上方，然后调整保温伞，使保温伞和地面平行。First, hang a brooder using an iron bar above the fence, and then adjust the brooder to ensure it is parallel to the ground.

2 Wǒmen shǒuxiān jìnrù xǐzǎojiān xǐzǎo, ránhòu jìnrù gēngyīshì chuān gōngzuòfú hé gōngzuòxié.
我们首先进入洗澡间洗澡，然后进入更衣室穿工作服和工作鞋。We first go into the bathroom to take a shower, and then go into the locker room to put on the working clothes and working shoes.

3 Wǒ shǒuxiān qīnglǐ lājī, ránhòu yízǒu bǎowēndēng, bǔliàocáo děng shèbèi.
我首先清理垃圾，然后移走保温灯、补料槽等设备。First, I cleared away rubbish, and then removed equipment like heat lamps, supplemental feeding troughs.

语法练习 1 Grammar Exercise 1

用“首先……，然后……”完成句子。Complete the sentences with “首先……，然后……”.

1 大卫　把红外线灯泡安装在灯头上　盖好铁丝网罩

____

2 我　消毒需要采样的水龙头　打开水龙头放水

____

3 他　用消毒液擦拭随身物品　用紫外线灯消毒

____

4 我　用扫帚清扫地板　用铁铲清理污物

____

语法点 2 Grammar Point 2

比较句：A 比 B + 形容词　Comparative sentence: A 比 B + 形容词

表示 A 在某方面的程度高过 B。

It indicates A is superior to B in a certain aspect.

常用结构：A + 比 + B+ 形容词

Common structure: A + 比 + B + adjective

例句：

1 Bǎowēnsǎn de xuánguà gāodù bǐ bǎowēndēng dī.
保温伞的悬挂高度比保温灯低。The brooder should be hung at a height lower than that of the heat lamp

2 Zhège liàocáo bǐ nàge liàocáo gānjìng.
这个料槽比那个料槽干净。This feeding trough is cleaner than that one.

3 Dàwèi bǐ wǒ gāo.
大卫比我高。David is taller than me.

语法练习 2 Grammar Exercise 2

把"比"放在句中合适的位置。Put "比" in the right place of the sentence.

1. 我们的养殖场____你们的养殖场____大。
2. 这个料桶____那个料槽____干净。
3. 大卫____我____高。
4. 宿舍楼____温度____办公楼温度高。

汉字书写 Writing Chinese Characters

huā 花

cǎo 草

miáo 苗

chá 茶

文化拓展 Culture Insight

The Spring Festival

The Spring Festival is one of the most grand and distinctive traditional festivals in China, generally referring to the New Year's Eve and the first day of the lunar new year, which is commonly known as "celebrating the New Year". With a long history, it originated from the primitive beliefs and natural worship of early humans, evolving from the sacrificial offerings and prayers for a good year in ancient times. As an original religious ceremony, people held sacrificial activities at the beginning of the year, praying for a bumper crop and prosperity of people and animals in the coming year. Over time, these activities gradually transformed into various celebration activities, ultimately shaping the Spring Festival into what it is today.

小结 Summary

词语 Words

朗读词语。Read the words aloud.

保温伞	首先	根	铁条	调整
悬挂	平行	高度	比	距离
平台	类型	发热管		

语法 Grammar

语言点回顾。Language points review.

语言点	常用结构	例句
承接复句：首先……，然后……	S + 首先 + P_1，然后 + P_2	他首先把保温伞用一根铁条悬挂在围栏上方，然后调整保温伞，使保温伞和地面平行。 我们首先进入洗澡间洗澡，然后进入更衣室穿工作服和工作鞋。
比较句：A 比 B + 形容词	A + 比 + B + Adj	保温伞的悬挂高度比保温灯低。 这个料槽比那个料槽干净。

课文理解 Text Comprehension

根据提示复述课文。Retell the text according to the prompts.

首先把保温伞用一根铁条悬挂在围栏________，然后调整保温伞，使保温伞和地面________。保温伞的悬挂高度比保温灯________，距离养殖平台大约25—30厘米。根据保温伞的类型，安装红外线________或者加热管。最后连接电源，打开________，调节________。

读者意见反馈

为收集对教材的意见建议，进一步完善教材编写并做好服务工作，读者可将对本教材的意见建议通过如下渠道反馈至我社。

咨询电话　0086-10-58581350

反馈邮箱　xp@hep.com.cn

通信地址　北京市西城区德外大街 4 号

高等教育出版社海外出版事业部（国际语言文化出版中心）

邮政编码　100120